THE SCHOOL MATHEMA...
PROJECT

When the S.M.P. was founded in 1961, its ... radically new mathematics courses, with accompanying ... buses and examinations, which would reflect, more adequately than did the traditional syllabuses, the up-to-date nature and usages of mathematics.

The first stage of this objective is now more or less complete. *Books 1–5* form the main series of pupils' texts, starting at the age of 11+ and leading to the O-level examination in 'S.M.P. Mathematics', while *Books 3T, 4* and *5* give a three-year course to the same O-level examination. (*Books T* and *T4*, together with their Supplement, represent the first attempt at this three-year course, but they may be regarded as obsolete.) *Advanced Mathematics Books 1–4* cover the syllabus for the A-level examination in 'S.M.P. Mathematics' and in preparation are five (or more) shorter texts covering the material of various sections of the A-level examination in 'S.M.P. Further Mathematics'. There are two books for 'S.M.P. Additional Mathematics' at O-level. Every book is accompanied by a Teacher's Guide.

For the convenience of schools, the S.M.P. has an arrangement whereby its examinations are made available by every G.C.E. Examining Board, and it is most grateful to the Secretaries of the eight Boards for their cooperation in this. At the same time, most Boards now offer their own syllabuses in 'modern mathematics' for which the S.M.P. texts are suitable.

By 1967, it had become clear from experience in comprehensive schools that the mathematical content of the S.M.P. texts was suitable for a much wider range of pupil than had been originally anticipated, but that the presentation needed adaptation. Thus it was decided to produce a new series, *Books A–H*, which could serve as a secondary school course starting at the age of 11+. These books are specially suitable for pupils aiming at a C.S.E. examination; however, the framework of the C.S.E. examinations is such that it is inappropriate for the S.M.P. to offer its own examination as it does for the G.C.E.

The completion of all these books does not mean that the S.M.P. has no more to offer to the cause of curriculum research. The team of S.M.P. writers, now numbering some thirty school and university mathematicians, is continually testing and revising old work and preparing for new. At the same time, the effectiveness of the S.M.P.'s work depends, as it always has done, on obtaining reactions from active teachers—and also from pupils—in the classroom. Readers of the texts can therefore send their comments to the S.M.P. in the knowledge that they will be warmly welcomed.

Finally, the year-by-year activity of the S.M.P. is recorded in the annual Director's Reports which readers are encouraged to obtain on request to the S.M.P. Office at Westfield College, University of London, Kidderpore Avenue, Hampstead, London NW3 7ST.

ACKNOWLEDGEMENTS

The principal authors, on whose contributions the S.M.P. texts are largely based, are named in the annual Reports. Many other authors have also provided original material, and still more have been directly involved in the revision of draft versions of chapters and books. The Project gratefully acknowledges the contributions which they and their schools have made.

This book – *Book G* – has been written by

> Joyce Harris   R. W. Strong
> D. A. Hobbs   Thelma Wilson
> K. Lewis

and edited by Elizabeth Smith.

The Project owes a great deal to its Secretary, Miss Jacqueline Sinfield, for her careful typing and assistance in connection with this book.

We would especially thank Professor J. V. Armitage for the advice he has given on the fundamental mathematics of the course.

Some of the drawings at the chapter openings in this book are by Ken Vail.

We are much indebted to the Cambridge University Press for their cooperation and help at all times.

THE SCHOOL MATHEMATICS PROJECT

BOOK G

CAMBRIDGE
AT THE UNIVERSITY PRESS   1971

Preface

This is the seventh of eight books primarily designed to cover a course suitable for those pupils who wish to take a C.S.E. examination on one of the reformed mathematics syllabuses. However, there are now three extension books in preparation with potential O-level candidates in mind. These books will lead on from *Book G* (thereby forming a ten book course) and will cover the syllabus of the O-level examination in 'S.M.P. Mathematics'.

For reasons already explained, we have purposely delayed the introduction of a manufactured slide rule until this stage. The slide rule chapter is placed early in the book and subsequent chapters provide opportunity for further practice. These are The Circle (which introduces π and is a sequel to the *Book E* chapter), Formulas and Trigonometry. Apart from containing more difficult computation work, the latter chapter deals with triangles in positions other than the familiar first quadrant one. Sines and cosines of angles greater than 90° are considered in Chapter 10, Waves.

The chapter, Paths of Moving Points, is entirely practical and consists of a series of carefully planned investigations. Work on the shearing transformation in Chapter 5 is also kept as practical as possible. In Chapter 8, we meet the shear transformation again and find that it, like other transformations we met in *Book F*, can be described algebraically by means of a matrix. This chapter also looks at the multiplicative inverses of certain matrices by considering inverse transformations.

Book G contains the final chapter on the popular topic of probability and involves the use of tree diagrams. This book also contains the last chapters of the *A–H* course on The Solution of Equations and Formulas. The latter chapter extends previous work on the substitution in and use of formulas and includes the formation of simple formulas, thereby paving the way for the Linear Programming chapter in *Book H*.

Answers to exercises are not printed at the end of this book but are contained in the companion Teacher's Guide which gives a detailed commentary on the pupil's text. In this series, the answers and commentary are interleaved with the text.

Contents

Contents

Prelude – Calculating

```
         36
         36
         36
         36
         36
         36
         36
         36
         36
         36
         36
         36
         36
         36
         36
         36
         36
         36
         36
         36
         36
         36
         36
         36
         36
         36
         36
         36
         36
         36
         36
         36
         36
         36
         36
         36
       1332
```

1. METHODS

How many ways can you think of for carrying out the multiplication 36×37? If you had never learnt any short ways, you would have to do it by the long and tedious method above.

The usual way is:

```
    36   or     36
  × 37        × 37
   252        1080
  1080         252
  1332        1332
```

In either case, you multiply by 7 and by 30 and then add up.

Do not turn over until you have tried to find some more methods of your own.

1

1.1 Other possible methods

(*a*) $36 \times 40 = 1440$

$\quad -36 \times 3\ = -108$ Here we really calculate thirty-six forties

$\qquad\qquad\qquad \overline{1332}$ and take away thirty-six threes.

(*b*) $36 \times 10 = 360$

$\quad 36 \times 10 = 360$ This method is very easy to do and is just

$\quad 36 \times 10 = 360$ as quick as the usual way.

$\quad 36 \times 5 = 180$

$\quad 36 \times 2 = 72$

$\qquad\qquad\quad \overline{1332}$

(*c*) Can you see what is happening below?

$$36 \times 37$$

can be written as

$$18 \times 74$$

and this can be written as

$$9 \times 148$$

which gives

$$1332.$$

(*d*) Look at Figure 1.

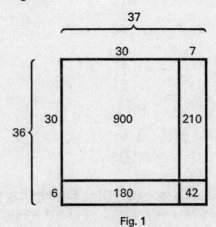

Fig. 1

The area of the rectangle is 36×37, or, if we consider the parts,

$$30 \times 30 = 900$$
$$30 \times 7 = 210$$
$$6 \times 30 = 180$$
$$6 \times 7 = 42$$
$$\text{Total} = \overline{1332}$$

We can write this as:

$$(30+6) \times (30+7) = (30 \times 30) + (30 \times 7) + (6 \times 30) + (6 \times 7)$$
$$= \quad 900 \quad + \quad 210 \quad + \quad 180 \quad + \quad 42$$
$$= 1332.$$

(*e*) Use a desk calculator. Does this make use of any of the above methods?

(*f*) Use a slide rule. Does this make use of any of the above methods?

See if you can think of any other methods or variations.

Try some of the methods given to calculate

(i) 32×24;　　(ii) 128×49;　　(iii) 83×56.

Since very early times men have tried to speed up calculations both by looking for quick methods and by inventing devices and machines to do the job.

Early number systems made little or no use of place value, that is, numbers were not written in columns of hundreds, tens and units. This made calculation more difficult than it is today. It is said that the Egyptians managed to do all their multiplication by doubling. For example:

13×7 would be done as

1	7
~~2~~	~~14~~
4	28
8	56
13	91

Can you see why the 2 and the 14 have been crossed out?

Copy the next example, cross out the numbers you do not need and complete the second column.

35×34 would be done as

1	34
2	68
4	136
8	272
16	544
32	1088
35	

What do you think of this method? Test it out by calculating 17×32 with a partner, one doing it the Egyptian way and the other doing it by the usual method, and see which is the quicker. You will really need to try many other pairs of numbers before you can make a worthwhile assessment of this method.

2. DEVICES

2.1 Fixed scales

You will already have made your own slide rule during this course. Figure 2 shows another pair of scales which can be used for multiplying. The red lines show the multiplication $4 \times 3 = 12$.

To use these scales for multiplying, find the first number on scale A, then go to 1 on scale B. Next go along scale B to the second number and from it draw a line parallel to the first line. The answer is at the point where the second line cuts scale A.

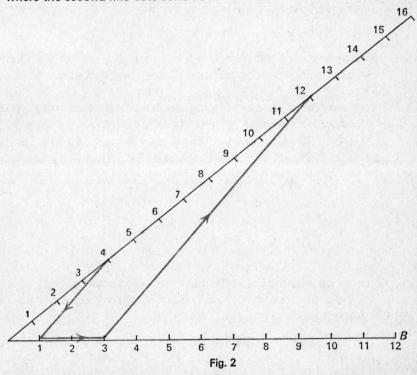

Fig. 2

How do the divisions on these scales differ from those of the slide rule? Does the angle between the two scales matter? Do the scales have to stop at 12 and 16? Need the steps be the same on both scales? Can intermediate divisions be marked?

When you have considered all these questions and experimented to find the answers, make yourself a large and accurate pair of scales.

How are you going to ensure parallel lines?

One way is to use a ruler and slide along a set square (see Figure 3) or anything with two adjacent straight edges. The parallel lines are shown in red.

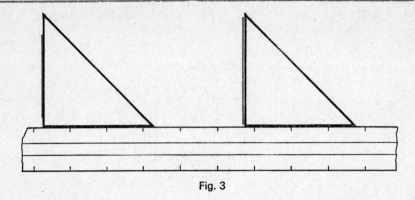

Fig. 3

Compare and contrast the usefulness of the device in Figure 2 with the slide rule.

The fixed scales make use of enlargement. In the example chosen, can you see the triangle which is enlarged with scale factor 3?

2.2 Napier's bones

Copy Figure 4 onto card and cut out so that you have the index strip and ten other separate strips 0, 1, ..., 9.

Index	0	1	2	3	4	5	6	7	8	9
1	0/0	0/1	0/2	0/3	0/4	0/5	0/6	0/7	0/8	0/9
2	0/0	0/2	0/4	0/6	0/8	1/0	1/2	1/4	1/6	1/8
3	0/0	0/3	0/6	0/9	1/2	1/5	1/8	2/1	2/4	2/7
4	0/0	0/4	0/8	1/2	1/6	2/0	2/4	2/8	3/2	3/6
5	0/0	0/5	1/0	1/5	2/0	2/5	3/0	3/5	4/0	4/5
6	0/0	0/6	1/2	1/8	2/4	3/0	3/6	4/2	4/8	5/4
7	0/0	0/7	1/4	2/1	2/8	3/5	4/2	4/9	5/6	6/3
8	0/0	0/8	1/6	2/4	3/2	4/0	4/8	5/6	6/4	7/2
9	0/0	0/9	1/8	2/7	3/6	4/5	5/4	6/3	7/2	8/1

Fig. 4

These can be used as a model of Napier's bones which were invented in 1617 by John Napier.

In Figure 5, the bones are set up to perform the multiplication
$$3 \times 65 = 195.$$

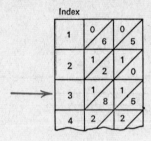

Fig. 5

Can you see how the answer is found?
Try the following:

(a) 2×32;   (b) 7×76;   (c) 5×65;

(d) 6×307;   (e) 23×56 (Hint: $23 = 20 + 3$.);

(f) 47×64;   (g) 326×458.

What else would be needed to perform a calculation such as 3×655?

2.3   Using the gelosia

Gelosia is an Italian word meaning grid. Grid multiplying was popular in the fifteenth to seventeenth centuries.

Study the grids in Figure 6 and find out how they show that
$$34 \times 45 = 1530.$$

  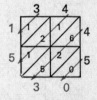

Fig. 6

Can you see how these numbers are obtained from *parts* of Napier's bones?

Copy and complete this gelosia:

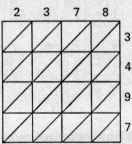

Fig. 7

Make new grids to do the following:

(a) 52×67; (b) 27×321; (c) 306×520; (d) 7642×5638.

3. DIVISION

All the work done so far in this Prelude has been concerned with multiplication, but what about division? Can we just reverse the methods used for multiplication and use them for division?

The first method of multiplication, used on p. 1, was repeated addition. The calculation $24 \div 6$ can be done by repeated subtraction:

$$
\begin{array}{r}
24 \\
- \ 6 \\
\hline
18 \\
- \ 6 \\
\hline
12 \\
- \ 6 \\
\hline
6 \\
- \ 6 \\
\hline
0 \\
\hline
\end{array}
$$

6 has been taken away 4 times and the answer to $24 \div 6$ is 4.

See what other methods you can discover for division. Can Napier's bones or a grid be used?

Exercise

1 Use repeated addition to find 27×17.

2 Find 183×99 by a short method.

3 Illustrate 56×73 by a diagram showing areas.

4 Use the Egyptian method to calculate 23×45.

5 Use Napier's bones to find:

    (a) 8×567;   (b) 25×73;   (c) 108×369.

6 Draw a grid to perform:

    (a) 46×77;   (b) 62×523;   (c) 4357×12584.

7 Find by repeated subtraction:

    (a) $256 \div 16$;   (b) $157 \div 24$.

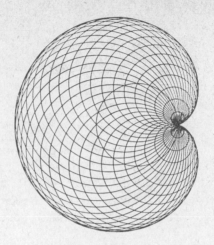

1. Paths of moving points

1. LINKAGES

You will need some strips of thick card or plastic or metal (for example, meccano) and some means of fixing them together such as paper fasteners, drawing pins, nuts and bolts.

Investigation 1

Take a strip about 20 cm long. Pin one end firmly to a sheet of paper on a drawing board (see Figure 1). Put a pencil point through a small hole at the other end. Rotate the strip about the pin. What is the path of the pencil point?

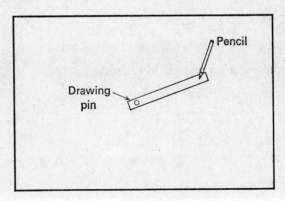

Pencil

Drawing
pin

Fig. 1

Investigation 2

You will need another strip the same length as the one in Investigation 1, and also a strip about twice as long.

Arrange the strips as shown in Figure 2. They are fixed to the board at *A* and *B* with drawing pins. The strips are linked at *C* and *D* with paper fasteners or nuts and bolts.

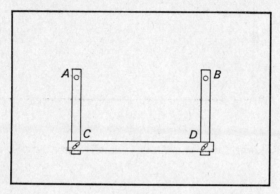

Fig. 2

(*a*) Make a hole in the middle of *CD* and put a pencil point through it. Move the strips so that *CD* stays parallel to *AB*. What is the path of the pencil point?

Try the pencil point in another hole which is not in the middle of *CD*.

(*b*) Move the drawing pins at *A* and *B* so that the distance between them is greater than *CD* (see Figure 3). Put the pencil point through the middle of *CD* and find the path which it traces out.

Try the pencil in other holes also.

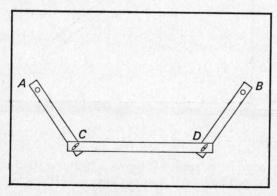

Fig. 3

(*c*) Move the strips so that *CD* is not parallel to *AB* (see Figure 4). Use the pencil to find the paths of some points on *CD*.

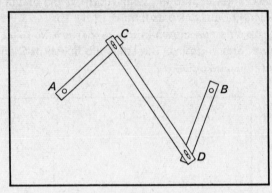

Fig. 4

(*d*) Try some more variations yourself; for example, alter the length of *AC*.

Investigation 3

Take two strips, not necessarily equal in length. Pin one end of each to a board and make holes at the other ends.

Bring these ends together and put a pencil point through them (see Figure 5). Try to move the pencil around. What do you find?

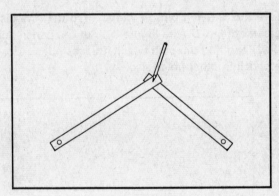

Fig. 5

Investigation 4

You have been investigating *linkages,* which are often used in everyday objects. Find out how they are used in some pedal bins.

Try to find some other examples of linkages.

2. UNDER THE INFLUENCE OF GRAVITY, OR THE DANGERS OF WINDOW CLEANING

(*a*) A window-cleaner is standing three-quarters of the way up a ladder. The ladder slips down the wall and the window-cleaner clings on to the ladder. See Figure 6.

Does he fall in a straight line? Or in a curve?

Describe what you think happens.

Fig. 6

(*b*) To find out more accurately what happens, draw two lines at right-angles in the middle of a page. Suppose we represent the ladder by a line of length 8 cm; then the window-cleaner would be 2 cm from the top. Place your ruler as shown in Figure 7 and mark a black dot for the position of the window-cleaner. Draw about ten more positions including one with the ladder vertical, keeping the red dots on the axes.

Repeat with 'ladders' in the other three parts of the diagram.

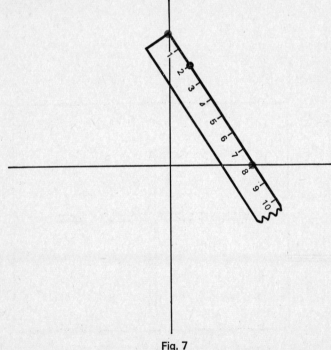

Fig. 7

11

(*c*) Repeat for other positions of the window-cleaner on the ladder; for example, a quarter of the way up, and half the way up. (The zero mark on the ruler must be on the axis up the page.)

(*d*) Next, draw in positions of the ladder as in Figure 8. You will need to draw at least ten lines. Repeat in the other three parts of the diagram. You should find that the lines you have drawn form a curve.

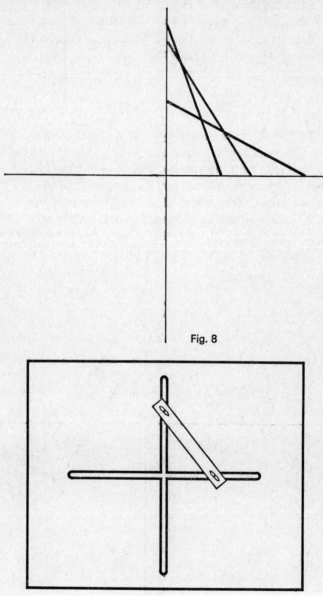

Fig. 8

Fig. 9

(*e*) You can make a model for this problem by using a strip of card and a large piece of card with two narrow slits in it. Fix the strip of card with paper fasteners so that the heads of the fasteners run in the slits. See Figure 9.

Make holes at several points in the strip large enough to put a pencil point through.

Choose one point, move the strip and so draw the path of the window-cleaner. Repeat for other positions of the window-cleaner on the ladder.

(*f*) You should have found that when the window-cleaner stands in the middle of the ladder his path is part of a circle. For any other position his path is part of a 'flattened' circle. This curve is called an *ellipse*.

The paths of the planets around the sun are approximate ellipses.

Another method of drawing an ellipse requires two drawing pins and a piece of thread. Stick the drawing pins into a board making them about 10 cm apart. Using about 30 cm of thread make a loop and put it around the pins. Stretch it out with the pencil point and move the pencil around. See Figure 10.

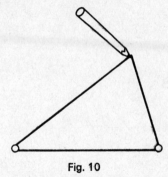

Fig. 10

3. ROLLING THINGS

Investigation 5

A square-ended box is being rolled across the floor without slipping. Figure 11 shows the starting position.

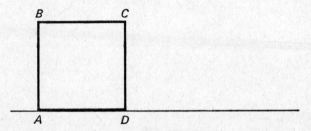

Fig. 11

First of all the box rotates about the corner *D*, and this causes the point *A* to move on a circular path as shown in Figure 12.

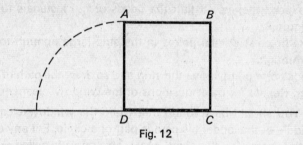

Fig. 12

With the help of compasses, draw the path of *A* from the position shown in Figure 11 until *A* is on the floor again.

Investigation 6

Repeat Investigation 5 with a rectangular-ended box.

Investigation 7

Try it now with an equilateral triangular-ended box (like a Toblerone chocolate box).

4. TRIANGLES

Investigation 8

(*a*) Mark two points *A* and *B* about 10 cm apart on a piece of tracing paper. Join them up by a line.

Fold the tracing paper so that *A* maps onto *B*. What can be said about the fold line and the line *AB* ?

Take any point *P* on the fold line. Join it to *A* and *B*. See Figure 13.

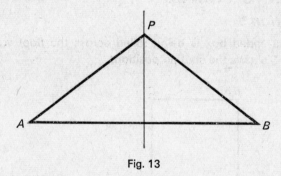

Fig. 13

What can be said about the lengths of *PA* and *PB* ? If in doubt fold the paper again so that *A* maps onto *B*.

(b) Spike, a mathematical spider, has to walk across the tracing paper so that his distance from A is always the same as his distance from B. Describe his route.

(c) Mark another point C on your paper. Join it up to A and B. See Figure 14.

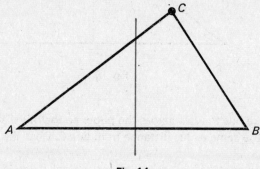

Fig. 14

By folding, find all the points which are equidistant from B and C.

Make another fold to find all the points which are equidistant from C and A.

Do your three folds meet at a point? If not, check the accuracy of your folding. Try to work out why they should meet at a point.

If Spike had to take up a position equidistant from A, B and C, where would he be?

(d) Using compasses, draw a circle which has its centre at this point and which passes through the vertices of the triangle ABC.

Investigation 9

(a) Draw a larger version of Figure 15 on tracing paper.

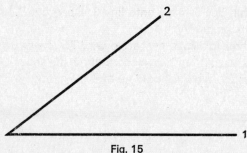

Fig. 15

Fold your tracing paper so that line 1 maps onto line 2.

Take any point on your fold line and join it at right-angles to each line as shown in Figure 16. What can be said about the lengths of PM and PN?

15

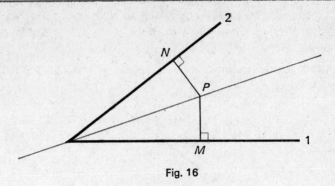

Fig. 16

(*b*) Spike has to walk across the paper so that his distance from line 1 is always the same as his distance from line 2. Describe his route.

(*c*) Draw another line on your paper and call it line 3. See Figure 17.

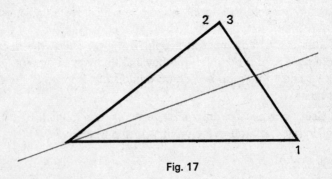

Fig. 17

Fold so that line 2 maps onto line 3. Open out. Make another fold so that line 3 maps onto line 1.

Do your three fold lines meet at a point? Try to work out why they should.

Spike has to position himself so that his distances from the three lines are all the same. Where should he be?

5. CURVES

Investigation 10

(*a*) Stick two drawing pins about 5 cm apart in a piece of paper on a wooden surface.

Cut a triangle out of card (any triangle that is not right-angled will do) and put it between the pins as shown in Figure 18.

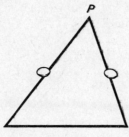

Fig. 18

Mark a dot for the position of the corner *P*. Move the triangle to a new position keeping the sides in contact with the pins. Repeat many times.

What shape do the dots make?

(*b*) Repeat with a right-angle corner of a triangle. You can use a set square if you wish.

Investigation 11

Figure 19 shows a double-ended searchlight.

Fig. 19

We are going to investigate the point of intersection of the beams when two searchlights are moved in various ways.

You will find it useful to have prepared sheets with lines marked at 10° intervals as in Figure 20 (over page).

17

Fig. 20

(*a*) The searchlight at *A* starts in the direction of *B*, while the one at *B* starts in the 60° direction (anticlockwise). (The starting rays are shown in red.) Both searchlights then rotate anticlockwise at the same speed, so that when the first is at 10° the second is at 70°, and so on.

Mark in the points of intersection of the beams. What curve do you obtain?

What can you say about the angle between the beams? Compare this with the path which you obtained in Investigation 10 (*a*).

(*b*) This time both beams start in the 0° direction, that is, across the page. They then rotate, but searchlight *B* goes twice as fast as *A*, so that when *A* is at 10°, *B* is at 20°, and so on. Mark in the points of intersection of the beams. What curve do you obtain?

(*c*) Both searchlights start in the 0° direction, but they rotate at the same speed in opposite directions. What curve do you obtain this time?

(*d*) The searchlights are rotated so that their angles always add up to 200°. (For example, when searchlight *A* is at 30°, *B* is at 170°.) What curve or curves do you obtain?

(*e*) Invent a method of your own for rotating the searchlights and see what curve you obtain.

6. MORE CURVES

The path of a moving point is called the *locus* of the point. It is usual to think of a curve being made out of points, but it is also possible to make up a curve using straight lines or even circles.

You have probably done some curve stitching before and made the curve shown in Figure 21. It is called a *parabola*. Notice that it is made up of straight lines. The path produced by a moving line is called an *envelope*.

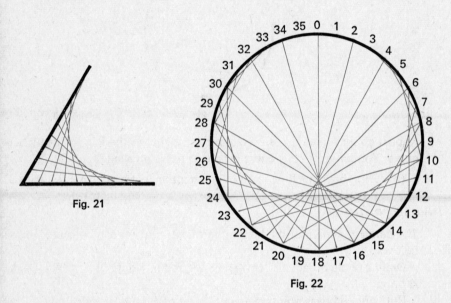

Fig. 21

Fig. 22

Figure 22 shows another curve made up of straight lines. It is called a cardioid. You may have met it before when doing curve-stitching.

Investigation 12

Here is another way of drawing a parabola.

Draw a line and mark a point *A* about 3 cm from it. See Figure 23. Place a set square *PQR* so that *P* is on the line and one side passes through *A*. Draw several positions of *PQ*. You will have to turn the set square over in order to get some positions below the level of *A*.

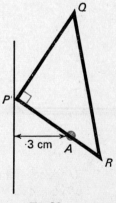

Fig. 23

Investigation 13

Obtain a circular piece of paper such as a filter paper.

(*a*) Mark a point *A* inside the circle, and fold the paper so that the circle passes through *A*. See Figure 24.

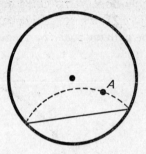

Fig. 24

Repeat about fifteen times. You should find that all the fold lines touch a curve. You have met this curve before. What is it called?

(*b*) What happens if you move *A* nearer the centre or nearer the edge?

Investigation 14

The cardioid shown at the beginning of this chapter can be obtained as follows:

Draw a circle of radius 3 cm (shown in red in Figure 25). Mark a point *A* on it.

Put your compass point on any other point *P* on this circle and draw a circle which passes through *A*.

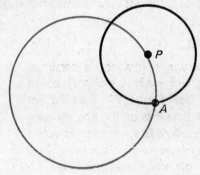

Fig. 25

Mark several more points spacing them equally around the red circle. Put your compass point on each point in turn, and each time draw a circle which passes through *A*.

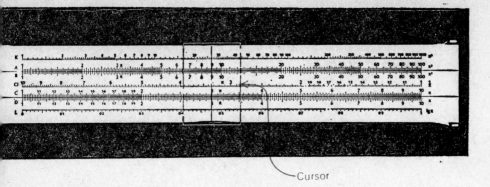

—Cursor

2. The slide rule

In *Book C* you made and used scales to carry out multiplications and divisions. In *Book E* you made slide rule scales using special graph paper which gave you more accurate answers to multiplications and divisions. What other two operations did you learn to do with your slide rule?

You will now find how to use a proper slide rule like the one above.

A manufactured rule has the advantages of being made very accurately and of having all the necessary scales. Study these scales carefully and make sure you understand them. Now try to write down any other advantages that you think a real slide rule has.

1. MULTIPLICATION

Follow the instructions in Figure 1 on your own slide rule to do the multiplication $2 \cdot 4 \times 3 \cdot 5$.

Rough check: $2 \cdot 4 \times 3 \cdot 5 \approx 2 \times 4 = 8$.

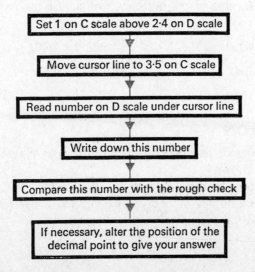

Set 1 on C scale above 2·4 on D scale

Move cursor line to 3·5 on C scale

Read number on D scale under cursor line

Write down this number

Compare this number with the rough check

If necessary, alter the position of the decimal point to give your answer

Fig. 1

The final position of the cursor and the C and D scales should be as shown in Figure 2.

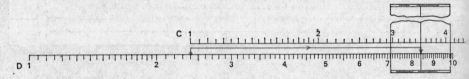

Fig. 2

Remember that if the answer to a multiplication is off the scale as it would be for, say, 4.6×3.8, then change ends. Instead of setting the 1 on the C scale, set the 10 on the C scale.

Exercise A

Remember to find a rough answer first. Try to give slide rule answers to 3 S.F. or to 2 S.F. depending on which end of the scale the answer comes.

1 1.6×3.5.	2 1.8×2.4.
3 7.6×9.2.	4 37×3.8.
5 0.83×14.	6 8.6×8.6.
7 1.48×1.8.	8 11.6×3.9.
9 7.25×0.91.	10 9.05×18.2.
11 1.7×11.2.	12 138×0.52.

In each of the last four questions there will not be an exact mark on your slide rule for one of the numbers. Set such a number as accurately as you can.

13 2.23×41.	14 22.7×1.46.
15 43.8×8.4.	16 5.17×730.

2. DIVISION

If you reversed the direction of the arrows in Figure 2, what division would be shown?

What would be the answer to this division?

Could you do any other divisions with the scales set in this position? If so, give some examples.

22

Follow the instructions in Figure 3 on your slide rule to do the division

$$36{\cdot}5 \div 7{\cdot}4.$$

Rough check: $36{\cdot}5 \div 7{\cdot}4 \approx 37 \div 7 \approx 5.$

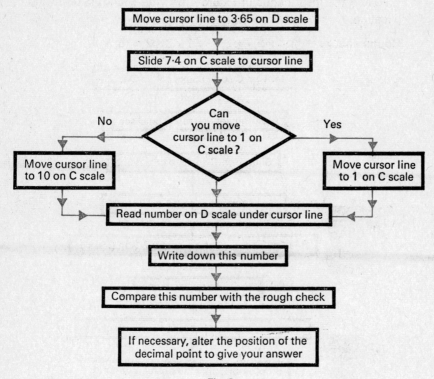

Fig. 3

Exercise B

Do not forget to find rough answers first.

1	$12{\cdot}6 \div 3{\cdot}4.$	2	$8{\cdot}4 \div 4{\cdot}2.$
3	$83 \div 6{\cdot}6.$	4	$5{\cdot}6 \div 9{\cdot}1.$
5	$840 \div 1{\cdot}2.$	6	$0{\cdot}5 \div 0{\cdot}125.$
7	$36{\cdot}5 \div 14{\cdot}7.$	8	$19{\cdot}8 \div 27{\cdot}5.$
9	$8{\cdot}6 \div 19{\cdot}2.$	10	$0{\cdot}3 \div 6{\cdot}4.$
11	$1{\cdot}4 \div 0{\cdot}9.$	12	$108 \div 24{\cdot}6.$
13	$335 \div 742.$	14	$0{\cdot}44 \div 2{\cdot}17.$
15	$7{\cdot}32 \div 4{\cdot}96.$	16	$62{\cdot}4 \div 301.$

3. MULTIPLICATION WITH MORE THAN TWO NUMBERS

The cursor is a great help in calculations involving three or more numbers.
Follow the instructions in Figure 4 on your slide rule to do the multiplication $1\cdot4 \times 2\cdot7 \times 2\cdot1$.

Rough check: $1\cdot4 \times 2\cdot7 \times 2\cdot1 \approx 1 \times 3 \times 2 = 6$.

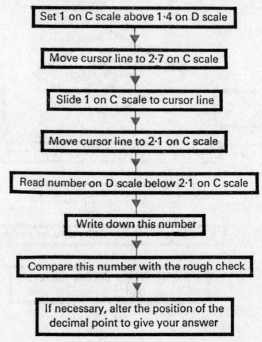

Set 1 on C scale above 1·4 on D scale

↓

Move cursor line to 2·7 on C scale

↓

Slide 1 on C scale to cursor line

↓

Move cursor line to 2·1 on C scale

↓

Read number on D scale below 2·1 on C scale

↓

Write down this number

↓

Compare this number with the rough check

↓

If necessary, alter the position of the decimal point to give your answer

Fig. 4

The final position of your cursor and the C and D scales should be as shown in Figure 5.

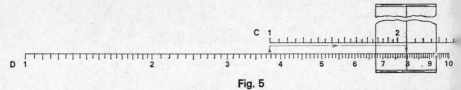

Fig. 5

When doing calculations involving three numbers, notice that the cursor line acts as a marker. In the example you have just completed it marked the answer to $1\cdot4 \times 2\cdot7$ (the first two numbers) and the position to which the 1 on the C scale had to be moved.

Exercise C

Remember to find a rough answer first.

1 $3\cdot1 \times 2\cdot5 \times 1\cdot1$.	2 $1\cdot7 \times 1\cdot9 \times 2\cdot1$.
3 $8\cdot6 \times 2\cdot5 \times 3\cdot7$.	4 $0\cdot5 \times 4 \times 4\cdot6$.
5 $15\cdot5 \times 2\cdot3 \times 7\cdot6$.	6 $0\cdot03 \times 15\cdot2 \times 17\cdot2$.
7 $1\cdot96 \times 2\cdot34 \times 1\cdot15$.	8 $(8\cdot4)^2 \times 1\cdot46$.
9 $17\cdot9 \times 1\cdot46 \times 2\cdot75$.	10 $1\cdot6 \times 2\cdot4 \times 0\cdot75 \times 3\cdot1$.
11 $3\cdot4 \times 2\cdot9 \times 14\cdot8 \times 0\cdot8$.	12 $2\cdot7 \times 5\cdot1 \times 3\cdot6 \times 9\cdot4 \times 1\cdot5$.

3.1 Multiplication and division

Method 1

Follow the instructions in Figure 6 on your slide rule to calculate $\dfrac{3\cdot6 \times 4\cdot2}{2\cdot5}$.

Rough check: $\dfrac{3\cdot6 \times 4\cdot2}{2\cdot5} \approx \dfrac{4 \times 4}{3} \approx 5$.

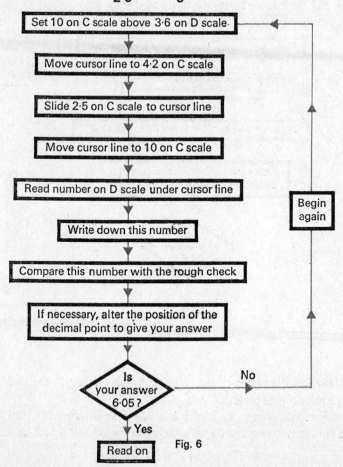

Set 10 on C scale above 3·6 on D scale.

Move cursor line to 4·2 on C scale

Slide 2·5 on C scale to cursor line

Move cursor line to 10 on C scale

Read number on D scale under cursor line

Write down this number

Compare this number with the rough check

If necessary, alter the position of the decimal point to give your answer

Is your answer 6·05?

Begin again

No

Yes

Read on

Fig. 6

25

Before attempting Method 2, do Questions 1, 2, and 3 of Exercise D.

Method 2

This time, follow the instructions in Figure 7 on your slide rule to calculate

$$\frac{3{\cdot}6 \times 4{\cdot}2}{2{\cdot}5}.$$

(Remember that the rough answer is 5.)

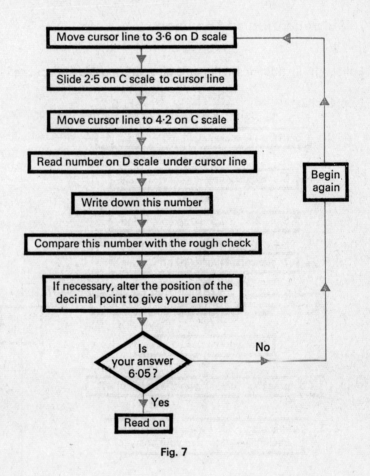

Fig. 7

How do the two methods differ? Which method is the shorter? Which
method do you prefer?

Repeat Questions 1, 2, and 3 of Exercise D using Method 2 and then
complete the exercise using whichever method you find easier.

Exercise D

1 $\dfrac{3\cdot5\times4\cdot2}{2}$.

2 $\dfrac{110\times9\cdot5}{8}$.

3 $\dfrac{18\cdot6\times6\cdot5}{7\cdot5}$.

4 $\dfrac{8\cdot6\times2\cdot4}{2\cdot5}$.

5 $\dfrac{34\times12}{1\cdot7}$.

6 $\dfrac{5\cdot2\times4\cdot3}{6\cdot6}$.

In some of the next six questions, if you use Method 2, you will have to mark the answer to the division (for example, $3\cdot7\div1\cdot5$ in Question 7) with the cursor and reset the sliding scale, that is, change ends.

7 $\dfrac{3\cdot7\times9\cdot6}{1\cdot5}$.

8 $\dfrac{17\cdot2\times1\cdot5}{9\cdot7}$.

9 $\dfrac{0\cdot61\times107}{25}$.

10 $\dfrac{3\cdot9\times1\cdot5}{20\cdot4}$.

11 $\dfrac{28\times21}{0\cdot625}$.

12 $\dfrac{384\times0\cdot543}{9\cdot5}$.

4. THE K SCALE

In *Book E* we compared the A and D scales. How are the numbers on scale A related to the numbers on scale D?

How are the numbers on scale D related to the numbers on scale A?

Find a rough answer and then use the A and D scales of your slide rule to work out:

(a) $(2\cdot5)^2$;

(b) $(5\cdot3)^2$;

(c) $\sqrt{18}$;

(d) $\sqrt{75}$;

(e) 36^2;

(f) $\sqrt{380}$.

On your slide rule you may have a K scale. Use your cursor to help you line up numbers on the K and D scales and then copy and fill in the following table:

Number on D scale	1	2		10	
Number on K scale			64		125

How are the numbers on the K scale related to the numbers on the D scale?

If the D scale is a one cycle scale and the A scale is a two cycle scale, what do you think the K scale could be called?

Use the K and D scales to work out:

(a) $(1\cdot7)^3$;

(b) $(2\cdot1)^3$;

(c) 24^3;

(d) $\sqrt[3]{8}$;

(e) $\sqrt[3]{64}$.

Exercise E (Miscellaneous)

Use your slide rule for all the calculations in this exercise. (Remember to find a rough answer first.)

1 (a) $3\cdot7 \times 4\cdot6$;   (b) $430 \times 31\cdot2$;   (c) $0\cdot632 \times 425$;

(d) $54\cdot5 \div 1\cdot96$;   (e) $7\cdot4 \div 36\cdot4$;   (f) $(16\cdot4)^2$;

(g) $(7\cdot6)^3$;   (h) $\sqrt{64}$;   (i) $\sqrt{145}$.

2 Evaluate the following:

(a) $2\cdot5 \times 18\cdot6 \times 12$;   (b) $35\cdot6 \div 8\cdot4$;

(c) $\dfrac{3\cdot6 \times 12\cdot4}{7\cdot5}$;   (d) $8\cdot2 \times 3\cdot4 \times \sqrt{27}$.

3 Find the areas of the following figures:

(a) a square of side 12·7 cm;

(b) a rectangle of sides 4·6 cm and 9·7 cm;

(c) an isosceles triangle of base 3·5 cm and height 7·3 cm;

(d) a circle of radius 2·8 cm. (The approximate area, A, of a circle of radius r is given by the relation $A = 3r^2$.)

4 Find the length of side of a cube whose volume is 512 cm³.

5 Find the surface area of a cube of side 3·6 cm. What is its volume?

6 In a school, the four houses Euler, Newton, Pascal and Pythagoras gained the following numbers of points throughout the year for the inter-house cup:

Euler	182
Newton	183
Pascal	287
Pythagoras	98

This information is to be represented by a pie chart. Calculate the angles.

7 A new aircraft is being designed with the following specifications:

Length overall	60 m
Wing span	26·8 m
Diameter of nose wheel	1·62 m
Height of cockpit roof above ground	8·6 m
Number of passengers	240
Number of crew	11
Maximum speed	950 knots

If a model of the aircraft is built on a scale of 1 to 72, what will be its specifications?

8   The prices of different sized boxes of chocolates are 15p, 27p, 39p, 50p. A price increase makes the largest box cost 60p. Write down the new prices if the other increases are in the same ratio.
     What will you do with fractions of a penny?

9   In a school the ratio of boys to girls is 4 to 5. There are 243 boys. How many girls are there? In a third form, there are 32 pupils; how many boys would you expect to find in this form?

10   At an annual sale the prices of all articles are reduced by 15%. What is the sale price of articles which normally cost
     (a) £5·20;   (b) £2;   (c) 55p;   (d) £12·70?

11   Take A, B and C in Figure 8 as the areas of the squares. Find the missing area in each case and then find the lengths of the sides of the triangle in each part.
     (a) $A = 16$ cm², $B = 7$ cm², $C = $ cm²;
     (b) $A = 28$ cm², $B = 16$ cm², $C = $ cm²;
     (c) $A = 30$ cm², $B = $ cm², $C = 50$ cm²;
     (d) $A = $ cm², $B = 67$ cm², $C = 225$ cm².

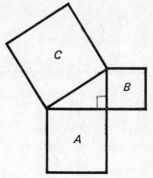

Fig. 8

5. INVESTIGATION: THE $\frac{1}{x}$ SCALE

You may have wondered about the middle scale on your slide rule. It is called the $\frac{1}{x}$ or reciprocal scale.

   Compare the $\frac{1}{x}$ scale with the C scale and write down any similarities or differences between them.
   Experiment to find a method for expressing $\frac{1}{5}$ as a decimal using the $\frac{1}{x}$ scale and the D scale. Test your method on some other fractions.

3. Probability

1. A REMINDER

(*a*) What is the probability of throwing a '5' with a die?

We know two ways of looking at this problem:

The experimental method

We can throw the die a large number of times and record the success fraction. If we throw the die 600 times and succeed in getting a '5' 103 times, we say that our success fraction is $\frac{103}{600}$. This success fraction gives an estimate of the probability.

The theoretical method

The set of possible outcomes is

$$P = \{1, 2, 3, 4, 5, 6\}$$

and the set of outcomes in which we are interested is

$$F = \{5\}.$$

If the die is a perfect cube (and is not loaded !) then we may reasonably suppose that we are equally likely to obtain any one of the six possible outcomes. We say that the probability of throwing a '5' is

the number of members of F

the number of members of P

which is sometimes written more briefly as

$$\frac{n(F)}{n(P)}.$$

Write down (i) $n(F)$;   (ii) $n(P)$;   (iii) $\dfrac{n(F)}{n(P)}$.

Do the two methods give approximately the same answer?

(b)   (i)   Put one red and three yellow counters in a box and, without looking, draw one out and note its colour. Put it back in the box, shake the box and repeat the experiment many times. What is your success fraction for drawing out a red counter?
(ii)   Use the theoretical method to find the probability of drawing a red counter from a box which contains one red and three yellow counters.
(iii)   Compare your answers to (i) and (ii). Does the second method help you to predict the result of the first method?

(c)   Use both the above methods to find the probability of throwing two heads with two coins. Compare your answers.

(d)   How would you find the probability that a drawing pin lands point up?

(e)   John throws a die 1200 times. His success fraction for obtaining a '6' is $\frac{461}{1200}$. What conclusion would you draw?

Exercise A

Find the probability of each of the events described in Questions 1–16.

1   Drawing a card from a pack and getting the ace of spades.

2   Drawing a card from a pack and getting a king.

3   Drawing a card from a pack and getting a diamond.

4   Drawing a card from a pack and not getting a diamond.

5 Drawing a card from a pack lackin g the seven of hearts and getting a spade.

6 Drawing a card from a pack lacking the seven of hearts and getting a heart.

7 Drawing a card from a pack lacking the seven of hearts and getting a seven.

8 Rolling a die and getting a number greater than 4.

9 Rolling a die and getting a number less than 9.

10 Rolling a die and getting a '7'.

11 Rolling a die and not getting a '6'.

12 Rolling a die with one red, two green and three blue faces and getting a green face.

13 Rolling a pair of dice and getting a total score of 10.

14 Rolling a pair of dice and not getting a total score of 10.

15 Tossing three coins and getting exactly two heads.

16 Tossing three coins and getting at least two heads.

17 What is the smallest value a probability can have ? What is the greatest value ?

18 If the probability that a person chosen at random is left-handed is $\frac{1}{20}$, what is the probability of being right-handed ?
How would you find the probability that a member of your school is left-handed ?

19 A coin is being tossed and heads have come up five times in succession. John claims that the probability of a tail on the next throw is greater than $\frac{1}{2}$. Do you agree ? Give a reason for your answer.

20 A die is to be rolled 600 times. About how many times would you expect a number greater than 2 to turn up ?

2. COMBINED EVENTS

Suppose we have two dice, a red one and a blue one, and that we roll both dice together. We can write each possible outcome as an ordered pair. For example, we shall write (2, 3) to mean a '2' on the red die and a '3' on the blue. We can then plot the ordered pairs as coordinates and show the possible outcomes on a diagram (see Figure 1).

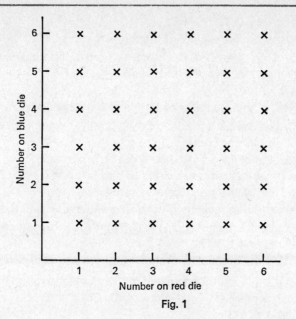

Fig. 1

How many possible outcomes are there? Are they all equally likely?

(*a*) (i) The set of outcomes which give a total score of 8 is

$$A = \{(2, 6), \quad (3, 5), \quad (4, 4), \quad (5, 3), \quad (6, 2)\}.$$

In Figure 2, a loop has been drawn round those crosses which represent members of *A*.

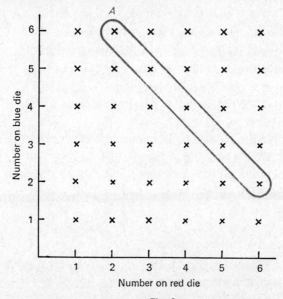

Fig. 2

What is $n(A)$?

What is the probability of throwing a total of 8?

(ii)   Copy Figure 2 and put another loop round those crosses which represent doubles. Call this set B.

What is $n(B)$?

What is the probability of throwing a double?

(iii)   List the set of outcomes which give *either* a total score of 8 *or* a double (or both).

List the members of $A \cup B$. What do you notice?

How many members has $A \cup B$, that is, what is $n(A \cup B)$?

Why is $n(A \cup B)$ not the same as $n(A) + n(B)$?

What is the probability of throwing either a total of 8 or a double?

(iv)   List the members of $A \cap B$. What does this set represent?

What is $n(A \cap B)$?

What is the probability of throwing *both* a total of 8 *and* a double?

(b)   (i)   Copy Figure 2 again and put another loop round those crosses which represent a total score of 11. Call this set C.

What is $n(C)$?

What is the probability of throwing a total of 11?

(ii)   What is $n(A \cap C)$?

What is the probability of throwing *both* a total of 8 *and* a total of 11?

(iii)   What is $n(A \cup C)$?

What is the probability of throwing *either* a total of 8 *or* a total of 11?

Explain why $n(A \cup C) = n(A) + n(C)$.

(c)   A card is chosen from a pack of 52 cards.

(i)   Let Q be the set of queens. What is $n(Q)$?

What is the probability of choosing a queen?

(ii)   Let B be the set of black cards. What is $n(B)$?

What is the probability of choosing a black card?

(iii)   What is $n(Q \cap B)$?

What is the probability of choosing a black queen?

(iv)   What is $n(Q \cup B)$? Be careful!

What is the probability of choosing either a queen or a black card (or both)?

Exercise B

1   Two dice are thrown together.

(a) Copy Figure 1 and put a loop round those crosses which represent ways of throwing a six on one die or the other (or both). Call this set S. Check that $n(S) = 11$.

(b) Put another loop round those crosses which represent ways of throwing a total of 10. Call this set *T*.

(c) Find (i) $n(S)$, (ii) $n(T)$, (iii) $n(S \cap T)$, (iv) $n(S \cup T)$.

(d) What is the probability of throwing:
- (i) at least one six;
- (ii) a total of 10;
- (iii) both a six and a total of 10;
- (iv) either a six or a total of 10 (or both)?

2 Two dice are thrown together. What is the probability of throwing:

(a) a total greater than 8;

(b) a double;

(c) either a double or a total greater than 8 (or both);

(d) both a double and a total greater than 8?

3 A penny and a die are tossed together. The possible outcomes are shown in Figure 3.

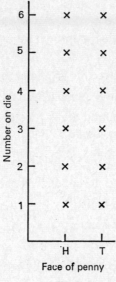

Fig. 3

(a) How many possible outcomes are there?

(b) What is the probability of getting a head?

(c) What is the probability of throwing a six?

(d) What is the probability of getting both a head and a six?

(e) What is the probability of getting either a head or a six (or both)?

4 The numbers 1 to 12 inclusive are placed in a hat and you draw a number without looking. What is the probability that

(*a*) the number is even;

(*b*) the number is divisible by 3;

(*c*) the number is either even or divisible by 3 (or both);

(*d*) the number is both even and divisible by 3?

  Suppose you draw a number, record it and replace it in the hat and that you repeat this experiment 600 times. Use your answer to (*d*) to predict your success fraction for obtaining a number which is both even and divisible by 3.

5 A card is drawn from a pack of 52 cards. What is the probability that it is

(*a*) a seven;

(*b*) a diamond;

(*c*) the seven of diamonds;

(*d*) either a seven or a diamond (or both)?

6 A red die and a blue die are thrown together. What is the probability that

(*a*) the number on the red die is greater than 5;

(*b*) the number on the blue die is less than 3;

(*c*) the number on the red die is greater than 5 and the number on the blue die is less than 3?

7 Figure 4 shows some dominoes. These are put face down on a table and a domino is chosen at random. What is the probability that

(*a*) it has at least one two;

(*b*) it has at least one blank;

(*c*) it has both a two and a blank;

(*d*) it has either a two or a blank (or both)?

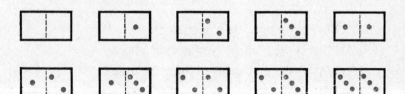

Fig. 4

3. TREE DIAGRAMS

(*a*) Suppose we throw two dice, a red one and a blue one, and that we want to know the probability of throwing

 (i) two sixes;

 (ii) exactly one six;

 (iii) no sixes.

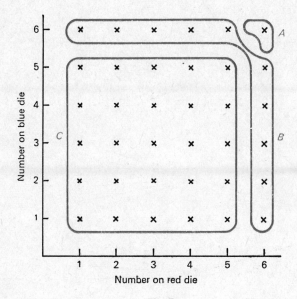

Fig. 5

Figure 5 shows the 36 possible outcomes. *A* is the set of ways of throwing two sixes, *B* is the set of ways of throwing exactly one six and *C* is the set of ways of throwing no sixes.

Write down (i) $n(A)$; (ii) $n(B)$; (iii) $n(C)$. Use your answers to help you to find the probability of throwing (i) two sixes; (ii) exactly one six; (iii) no sixes.

What is the sum of the three probabilities? Give an explanation for your answer.

In Figure 5, we plotted the ordered pairs which represent the 36 possible outcomes as coordinates. Instead we could show them as 'branches' of a 'tree':

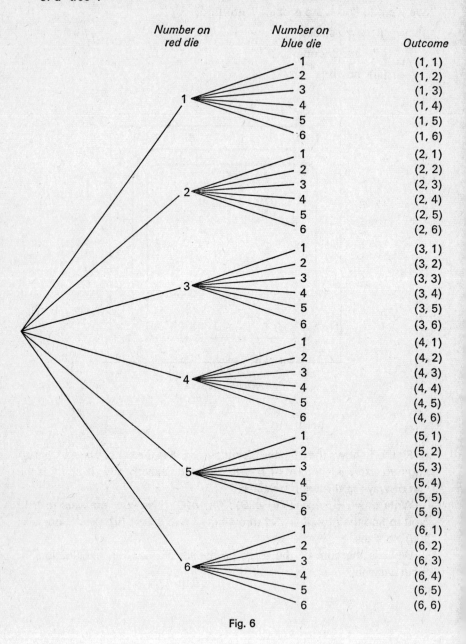

Fig. 6

Since we are interested only in the number of sixes we throw, we can draw a simpler *tree diagram* by stacking together the numbers 1, 2, 3, 4 and 5 and calling them 'not 6':

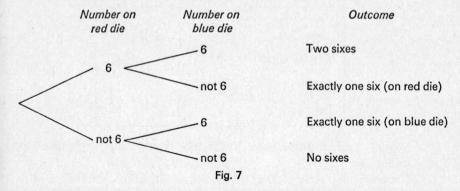

Fig. 7

Suppose we look first at the number on the red die. What is the probability that it is a six?

Let us now look at the number on the blue die. In $\frac{1}{6}$ of our experiments we shall expect a six and in the other $\frac{5}{6}$ of our experiments we shall not expect a six.

So, for example, in $\frac{1}{6}$ of $\frac{1}{6} = \frac{1}{36}$ of our experiments we shall expect to throw two sixes and in $\frac{5}{6}$ of $\frac{1}{6} = \frac{5}{36}$ of our experiments we shall expect to throw a six on the red die and some other number on the blue die.

Copy and complete Figure 8 by writing the appropriate probability on each branch of the tree. Some of the probabilities have been put in to help you.

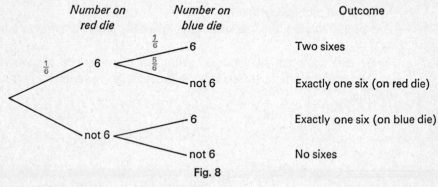

Fig. 8

Since the order in which we multiply numbers does not matter, we can obtain the probabilities of the outcomes by multiplying from left to right along the appropriate branches of the tree. For example, instead of saying that the probability of throwing exactly one six (on the red die) is

$$\frac{5}{6} \text{ of } \frac{1}{6} = \frac{5}{36},$$

39

we can say that it is $\frac{1}{6} \times \frac{5}{6} = \frac{5}{36}$.

Use this idea to copy and complete the following table:

Outcome	Probability
Two sixes	$\frac{1}{6} \times \frac{1}{6} = \frac{1}{36}$
Exactly one six (on red die)	$\frac{1}{6} \times \frac{5}{6} = \frac{5}{36}$
Exactly one six (on blue die)	
No sixes	

Add up the four probabilities in the table and give an explanation for your answer.

The completed table shows that the probability of throwing exactly one six (on the red die) is $\frac{5}{36}$ and the probability of throwing exactly one six (on the blue die) is $\frac{5}{36}$. If we do not mind whether the six is on the red or the blue die, the probability of throwing exactly one six is

$$\frac{5}{36} + \frac{5}{36} = \frac{10}{36} = \frac{5}{18}.$$

Does this answer agree with the one which you obtained from Figure 5?

How can you use the table to find the probability of throwing at least one six?

The outcomes in Figure 6 are all equally likely. Are the outcomes in Figure 8 all equally likely?

(*b*) There are 5 red balls and 2 white balls in a bag and a ball is drawn from the bag.

What is the probability that it is (i) red; (ii) white?

The ball is replaced, the bag is shaken and a ball is again drawn from the bag.

Copy and complete Figure 9 by writing the appropriate probability on each branch of the tree. Some of the probabilities have been put in to help you.

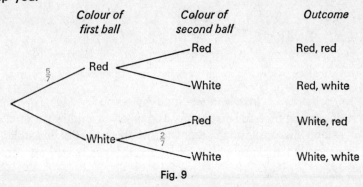

Fig. 9

Now copy and complete this table:

Outcome	Probability
Red, red	
Red, white	$\frac{5}{7} \times \frac{2}{7} = \frac{10}{49}$
White, red	
White, white	

What is the probability of drawing

    (i) 2 balls of different colours;

   (ii) 2 balls of the same colour?

(*c*) Suppose now that the second ball is replaced, the bag is shaken and a ball is again drawn from the bag.

Copy and complete Figure 10 by writing the appropriate probability on each branch of the tree diagram.

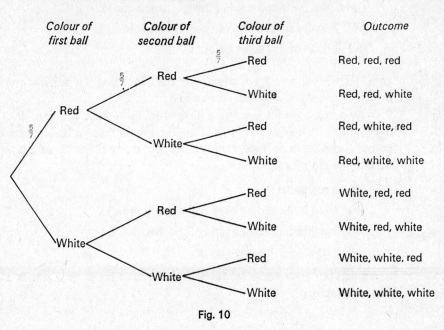

Fig. 10

Now copy and complete this table:

Outcome	Probability
Red, red, red	$\frac{5}{7} \times \frac{5}{7} \times \frac{5}{7} = \frac{125}{343}$
Red, red, white	$\frac{5}{7} \times \frac{5}{7} \times \frac{2}{7} = \frac{50}{343}$
Red, white, red	
Red, white, white	
White, red, red	
White, red, white	
White, white, red	
White, white, white	

What is the probability of drawing

    (i)   3 red balls;

    (ii) 2 red balls and a white ball (in any order);

    (iii) 2 white balls and a red ball (in any order);

    (iv) 3 balls of the same colour?

(*d*) Place 5 red and 2 white snooker balls in a bag. (If balls are not available, counters, all of the same size, will do.)

Draw a ball from the bag, note its colour and replace it. Again draw a ball, note its colour and replace it. Once more draw a ball, note its colour and replace it. Repeat this experiment many times. What is your success fraction for drawing:

    (i)   3 red balls;

    (ii) 2 red balls and a white ball (in any order);

    (iii) 2 white balls and a red ball (in any order);

    (iv) 3 balls of the same colour?

Would your answers to (*c*) have helped you to predict the results of this experiment?

Exercise C

1   Copy and complete the tree diagram in Figure 11 to show the possible outcomes for two tosses of a coin. Use it to find the probability of getting:

(*a*) 2 heads;   (*b*) 2 tails;   (*c*) 1 head and 1 tail.

Result of first throw	*Result of second throw*	*Outcome*
Head	Head	Head, head
	Tail	Head, tail
Tail	Head	Tail, head
	Tail	Tail, tail

Fig. 11

2   Draw a tree diagram to show the possible outcomes for three tosses of a coin. Use it to find the probability of getting:

(*a*) exactly two heads;   (*b*)   at least two heads.

Check that you get the same results as in Exercise A, Questions 15 and 16.

3   A card is drawn from a pack of fifty-two. It is then replaced and a card is again drawn. Copy and complete the tree diagram in Figure 12 and use it to find the probability of drawing:

(*a*) two aces;   (*b*) at least one ace.

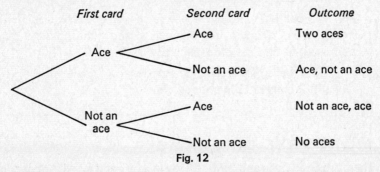

First card	*Second card*	*Outcome*
Ace	Ace	Two aces
	Not an ace	Ace, not an ace
Not an ace	Ace	Not an ace, ace
	Not an ace	No aces

Fig. 12

4   Place a pack of 52 cards face downwards. Pick out a card, look at it, note its suit and replace it. Again pick out a card, note its suit and replace it. Repeat this experiment many times. What is your success fraction for drawing:

(*a*) two spades;   (*b*) exactly one spade;   (*c*) no spades?

5 A card is selected from a pack of 52. It is then replaced and a card is again selected. By drawing a suitable tree diagram, find the probability of selecting:

(*a*) two spades; (*b*) exactly one spade; (*c*) no spades.

Would your answers have helped you to predict the result of your experiment in Question 4?

6 It is found that the probability that a particular brand of firework will not light is $\frac{1}{5}$.

John buys two. Copy and complete the tree diagram in Figure 13 and use it to find the probability that both of his fireworks light.

Anne buys three. By drawing a suitable tree diagram, find the probability that at least two of her fireworks light.

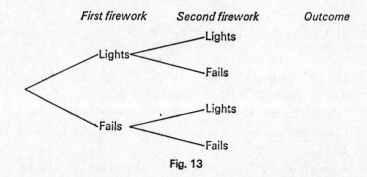

Fig. 13

7 (*a*) A bag contains 5 white balls, 3 blue ones and 2 red ones. A ball is drawn from the bag. What is the probability that the ball is (i) white; (ii) blue; (iii) red?

(*b*) The ball is replaced, the bag is shaken and a ball is again drawn from the bag. Draw a tree diagram to show the possible outcomes and use it to find the probability of drawing:

(i) 2 balls of the same colour;
(ii) 2 balls of different colours.

4. MORE TREE DIAGRAMS

There are 5 red balls and 2 white balls in a bag and a ball is drawn from the bag.

This time the first ball is not replaced before a second one is drawn.

Suppose that the first ball is red. How many of the 6 remaining balls are (i) red, (ii) white? If it is known that the first ball is red, what is the probability that the second ball is (i) red, (ii) white?

If it is known that the first ball is white, what is the probability that the second ball is (i) red, (ii) white?

Copy and complete Figure 14 by writing the appropriate probability on each branch of the tree.

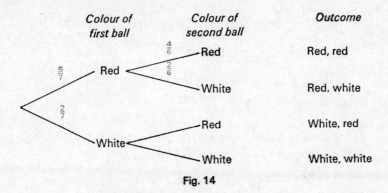

| Colour of first ball | Colour of second ball | Outcome |

Fig. 14

Now copy and complete this table:

Outcome	Probability
Red, red	$\frac{5}{7} \times \frac{4}{6} = \frac{20}{42} = \frac{10}{21}$
Red, white	$\frac{5}{7} \times \frac{2}{6} = \frac{10}{42} = \frac{5}{21}$
White, red	
White, white	

What is the probability of drawing
  (i) 2 balls of the same colour;
  (ii) 2 balls of different colours?

Exercise D

1   A box contains 7 red ball-point pens and 3 blue ones. Jane takes a pen from the box and keeps it; then Susan takes one also. Both girls make their selection without looking at the colour.

Copy and complete the tree diagram in Figure 15 and use it to find the probability that Jane and Susan

  (a) each select a red pen;
  (b) each select a blue pen;
  (c) select pens of the same colour;
  (d) select pens of different colours.

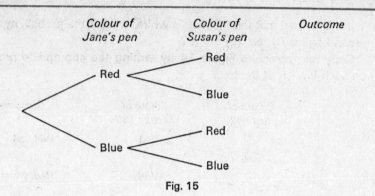

Fig. 15

2 (a) A card is drawn from a pack of fifty-two. What is the probability that it is an ace? How many cards remain?

(b) The first card drawn is an ace. How many aces are left? If another card is now drawn, what is the probability that it is also an ace?

(c) If it is known that the first card is not an ace and another card is drawn, what is the probability that the second card is an ace?

(d) Two cards are drawn one after the other from a pack. Draw a suitable tree diagram and use it to find the probability that:

    (i) they are both aces;
    (ii) at least one is an ace.

(e) Compare your answers with those which you obtained in Exercise C, Question 3. Are you more likely to draw two aces if you draw both cards together or if you replace the first card before drawing the second?

3 Two cards are drawn from a pack of fifty-two. By drawing a suitable tree diagram, find the probability of drawing:

(a) two spades;   (b) exactly one spade;   (c) no spades.

Compare your answers with those which you obtained in Exercise C, Question 5.

4 Place a pack of 52 cards face downwards. Pick out two cards, look at them, record their suits and replace them. Repeat this experiment many times. What is your success fraction for drawing:

(a) two spades;   (b) exactly one spade;   (c) no spades?

Would your answers to Question 3 have helped you to predict the results of this experiment?

5 A car may fail its road test on lights with probability $\frac{1}{3}$, on steering with probability $\frac{1}{2}$, and on brakes with probability $\frac{1}{4}$. Copy and complete the tree diagram in Figure 16 and use it to find the probability that a particular car will pass its test.
Why is it unnecessary to draw *all* the tree diagram?

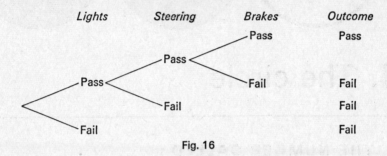

Fig. 16

6 (*a*) A box of twelve pens contains three which are defective. If one pen is bought, what is the probability that it is (i) good; (ii) defective?

(*b*) If it is known that the first pen is defective and another is bought, what is the probability that it is (i) good; (ii) defective?

(*c*) If it is known that the first pen is good and another is bought, what is the probability that it is (i) good; (ii) defective?

(*d*) I buy two pens from the box. By drawing a tree diagram, find the probability that I buy

(i) two good pens; (ii) two defective pens; (iii) one of each.

7 A bag contains 5 white balls, 3 blue ones and 2 red ones. Two balls are drawn from the bag. By drawing a tree diagram, find the probability of drawing:

(*a*) two balls of the same colour;

(*b*) two balls of different colours.

Compare your answers with those which you obtained for Exercise C, Question 7.

8 A box contains 100 transistors, 20 of them being defective.

(*a*) If one is taken from the box, what is the probability that it is a good one?

(*b*) If the first one is good and another is taken, what is the probability that it is (i) good, (ii) defective?

(*c*) By drawing a suitable tree diagram, find the probability that

(i) both are good;   (ii) both are defective;
(iii) there is exactly one good one.

47

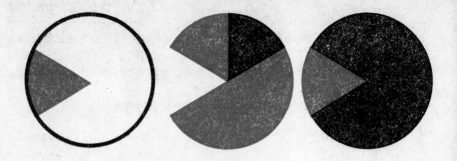

4. The circle

1. THE NUMBER CALLED π

In *Book E* we found that the circumference of a circle was three-and-a-bit times the diameter, and we used the approximate relation

$$C = 3d.$$

We are now going to look at this three-and-a-bit more closely.

The Babylonians and the ancient Jews thought that the bit did not matter. They used 3 as the multiplier. It is interesting to look this up in the Bible. Read the First Book of Kings, Chapter 7, verse 23.

The ancient Greeks worked very hard to find more accurate versions of this important number. Archimedes said that the true number lay between $3\frac{1}{7}$ and $3\frac{10}{71}$.

The Chinese used $3\frac{1}{7}$. This is quite a good approximation and is often used today.

Modern Mathematicians using electronic computers can work out the three-and-a-bit to many thousands of decimal places. Even then they can never find it exactly and must always give an approximation. It is impossible to find an exact fraction for this number. (Remember that this was also the case with most of the square roots we met in *Book E*.)
The three-and-a-bit is

3·14159265358979323846264338327950288419716939937510582097494459230781640628620899862803482534211706798214808651328230664709384460955058223172535940812...

and it goes on for ever. Is there any pattern? Can you tell what the next digit is?

It is no wonder that it is convenient to have a special name (pi) and a special symbol (π) for so unusual a number! In the Greek alphabet, π is equivalent to the letter p.

We can now write the relation between the circumference and the diameter as

$$C = \pi d.$$

We shall sometimes take the value of π as 3

or 3·1

or 3·14

or 3·142

or 3·1416

according to the accuracy of the work we are doing. A very useful value is $3\frac{1}{7} = \frac{22}{7}$. Convert this into a decimal and compare it with the values given above.

Remember that the value you take for π will always be an approximation.

Is there a special mark for π on your slide rule?

Here is a sentence which will help you to remember the value of π to six decimal places:

'How I wish I could calculate pi'
3   1   4   1   5   9   2

Exercise A

1 Take the value of π as 3·1 and use it to find the circumference of each of the circles in Figure 1.

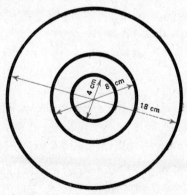

Fig. 1

2 Use your slide rule to calculate the circumferences of circles with the following diameters:

(a) 12·2 cm; (b) 58·8 m; (c) 36 mm; (d) 0·09 cm.

3 Use your slide rule to calculate the circumferences of circles with the following radii:

(a) 4·3 cm;   (b) 11 m;   (c) 1·05 km;   (d) 200 m.

4 Take the value of π as $\frac{22}{7}$ and calculate the circumferences of circles with the following dimensions:

(a) radius 14 m;   (b) diameter 3500 m;   (c) radius 2·1 km.

Why was the value of π taken as $\frac{22}{7}$ in each of these questions?

5 Since $C = \pi d$, $d = C \div \pi$. Use a slide rule to find the diameters of circles with the following circumferences:

(a) 88 cm;   (b) 4·5 cm;   (c) 5100 m;   (d) 25·7 cm.

6 A child's bicycle has wheels whose diameter, including the tyres, is 53 cm. What is the circumference of one of the wheels? How far forward does the bicycle go in 80 revolutions of the wheel?

7 The radius of a wheel is 1·032 m (to the nearest thousandth of a metre). Take 3·142 as your approximation to π and use long multiplication, or a desk calculator, to find the circumference of the wheel. To what accuracy do you think you should give your answer?

2. THE AREA OF A CIRCLE

Another approximate relation we found in *Book E* was for the area, A, of a circle of radius r: $A = 3r^2$.

This should really be

$$A = \text{three-and-a-bit} \times r^2,$$

and we now know that this is

$$A = \pi r^2.$$

Exercise B

1 Take π as $\frac{22}{7}$ and find the areas of circles with the following dimensions:

(a) radius 7 cm;   (b) radius 10·5 m;   (c) diameter 28 cm.

2 Take π as 3·14 and, without using a slide rule, find the areas of circles with the following dimensions:

(a) radius 3 cm;   (b) diameter 20 cm;   (c) radius 20 mm.

3 Use your slide rule to help find the areas of circles with the following dimensions:

(a) radius 2·6 cm;   (b) diameter 17 m;   (c) radius 1·05 km.

4   Find the total area of the four shaded regions in Figure 2.

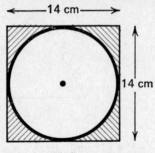

Fig. 2

5   A radar screen is circular and has a diameter of 42 cm. Taking the value of π to be $\frac{22}{7}$, find the area of the screen.

6   Make a collection of tin cans of circular cross-section. Measure the diameters of each of the circles and hence find their areas.

3. SECTORS

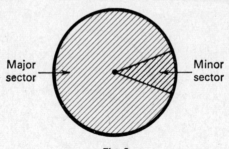

Fig. 3

When two radii are drawn, a circle is divided into two sectors as shown in Figure 3. Some sectors with special names are:

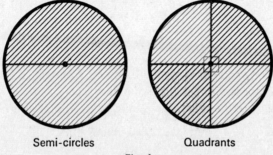

Semi-circles   Quadrants

Fig. 4

51

The simplest way of describing a sector is to give its radius and angle; for example:

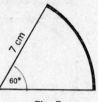

Fig. 5

(*a*) What is the circumference of a circle of radius 7 cm? What fraction of the circumference is the length of the arc in Figure 5? Hence calculate the length of the arc.

(*b*) What is the area of a circle of radius 7 cm? What fraction of a complete circle is the sector in Figure 5? Hence find the area of the sector.

(*c*) Copy and complete the following example and so find the length of the arc of a sector, angle 200°, cut from a circle of radius 3 cm (see Figure 6).

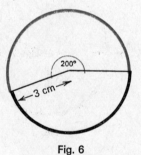

Fig. 6

200° corresponds to $\frac{200}{360}$ of a complete turn.
Length of the arc is therefore $\frac{200}{360}$ of complete circumference

$$= \frac{200}{360} \times \pi \times 6 \text{ cm}$$

$$= \qquad \text{cm.}$$

(*d*) Copy and complete the following example and so find the area of a 35° sector cut from a circle of radius 5 cm.
The area of the sector is $\frac{35}{360}$ of area of whole circle

$$= \frac{35}{360} \times \pi \times 5^2 \text{ cm}^2$$

$$= \qquad \text{cm}^2.$$

Exercise C

1 Take π as 3·14 and find the lengths of the arcs of the shaded sectors in Figure 7.

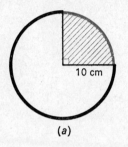
(*a*)

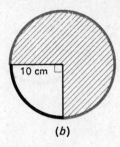
(*b*)

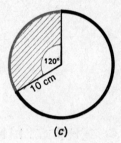
(*c*)

Fig. 7

2 Find the *total* perimeter of a sector of angle 72° cut from a circle of radius 7 cm. (See Figure 8.)

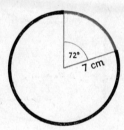

Fig. 8

3 Taking the value of π as 3·14, copy and complete the following table for a circle of radius 10 cm.

Angle (degrees)	Length of arc (cm)	Area of sector (cm²)
30		
60		
90		
120		

Comment on the relations between the sets of figures in the three columns.

4 Find the areas of sectors cut from a circle of radius 13 cm which have angles of:

(*a*) 31°; (*b*) 124°; (*c*) 236°.

5 What is the total length of all the arcs forming the petals in Figure 9 if the radius of the circle is 5 cm?

Fig. 9

4. THE CYLINDER

4.1 The volume of a cylinder

A cylinder is a prism of circular cross-section.

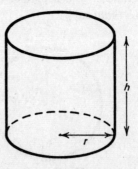

Fig. 10

In *Book E*, Chapter 9, you found that the volume of a prism whose end is made up of triangles and rectangles is given by the relation

$$\text{volume} = \text{area of base} \times \text{height}.$$

The same relation is true for a cylinder.

In Figure 10, what is the area of the base of the cylinder? What is the height?

Now try to complete the following relation for the volume, V, of the cylinder:

$$V = \qquad .$$

Exercise D

1 Use suitable values of π and find the volumes of cylinders with the following dimensions:

(a) base area 12 cm², height 4 cm;

(b) base radius 7 cm, height 6 cm;

(c) base diameter 20 cm, height 2·3 cm.

2 Take the value of π as 3·14 and find the volumes of the cylinders shown in Figure 11.
Did you expect the volumes to be equal? Explain what you find.

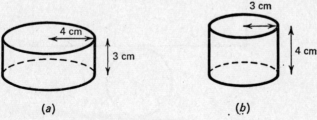

Fig. 11

3 Use your slide rule to find the volume of a cylinder of height 2·45 cm and base radius 0·55 cm.

4 The volume of a cylinder is 80 cm³ and the area of its base is 16 cm². What is the height of the cylinder?

5 A stick of seaside rock is cylindrical and has a volume of about 100 cm³. If the radius of the cylinder is 1 cm, how long is it?

4.2 The surface area of a cylinder

Draw the shapes shown in Figure 12 accurately on thin card, cut them out and see if you can assemble them with the aid of adhesive tape to make a cylinder.

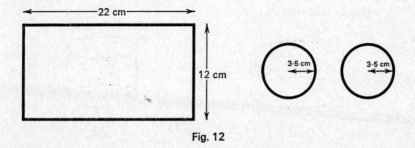

Fig. 12

How is the length of the long side of the rectangle related to the circumference of the circle?

How much card would be needed to make a cylinder of base radius *r* cm and height *h* cm? Figure 13 should help.

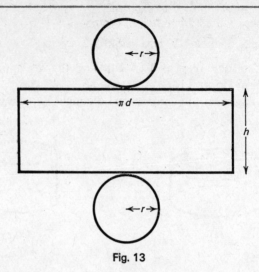

Fig. 13

What is the area of the *curved* surface of the cylinder?
What is the *total* surface area of the cylinder?

Exercise E

1   Take the value of π as $\frac{22}{7}$ and find the area of the curved surfaces of
cylinders with the following dimensions:

(*a*) diameter 28 cm, height 40 cm;

(*b*) radius 10·5 cm, height 18 cm;

(*c*) diameter 35 cm, height 35 cm.

2   Take the value of π as 3·14 and find the areas of the curved surfaces of
the cylinders shown in Figure 14.

Did you expect the areas of the curved surfaces to be equal? Explain what you find.

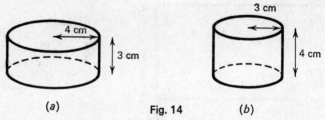

(*a*)   Fig. 14   (*b*)

3   Use your slide rule to find the area of the curved surface of a cylinder
of height 2·45 cm and base radius 0·55 cm.

4   Take the value of π as $\frac{22}{7}$ and find the total surface area of a cylinder
of height 10 cm and base radius 1·4 cm.

5 A water pipe on the side of a house has a radius of 6 cm and a length of 4·5 m. You have a tin of paint sufficient to cover 2 m². Is this enough to paint the whole pipe?

Summary

If we divide the circumference of a circle by its diameter we get the number called π.

π can never be calculated exactly.

π is sometimes taken as 3

or 3·1

or 3·14

or 3·142

or 3·1416

or $3\frac{1}{7} = \frac{22}{7}$.

The following relations are true for a cylinder with the measurements shown in Figure 15:

Circumference of circular end $= \pi d$.
Area of circular base $= \pi r^2$.
Volume of cylinder $= \pi r^2 h$.
Area of curved surface $= \pi dh$.

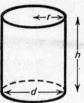

Fig. 15

Exercise F (Miscellaneous)

In Questions 1 and 2, take the value of π to be 3·14 or $\frac{22}{7}$, as you think appropriate.

1 Calculate the circumferences of circles with the following radii:

(a) 4 m;   (b) 7·0 cm;   (c) 5·24 cm.

2 Calculate the areas of circles with the following radii:

(a) 0·83 cm;   (b) 21 m;   (c) 1 km.

3 Taking the value of π as $\frac{22}{7}$, find the length of the arc cut off:

(a) from a circle of radius 35 cm by two radii at 60°;

(b) from a circle of radius 210 cm by two radii at 135°;

(c) from a circle of radius 1·4 m by two radii at 300°.

4 Use your slide rule to find the area of a sector:

(a) of angle 48° cut from a circle of radius 4·55 cm;

(b) of angle 240° cut from a circle of radius 2·03 m.

5   Find the areas of each of the shaded regions in Figure 16.

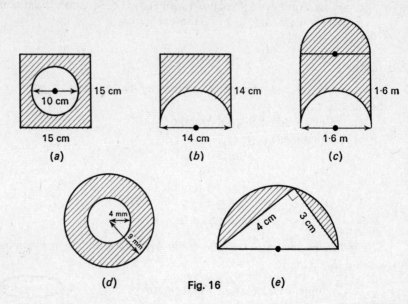

(a)   (b)   (c)

(d)   **Fig. 16**   (e)

6   The front wheel of a penny-farthing bicycle has three times the radius of the back wheel. How many times does the back wheel rotate while the front wheel turns round once?

7   Two circles have radii of 2 m and 3 m respectively.

(a) Write down expressions for (i) their circumferences and (ii) their areas, but do not work them out.

(b) Write down (i) the ratio of their circumferences and (ii) the ratio of their areas.

(c) A third circle has a radius of 5 m.
   (i) Write down the ratio of its circumference to that of the 2 m circle;
   (ii) write down the ratio of its area to that of the 2 m circle.

8   What is the ratio of the area of the shaded sector to that of the unshaded sector in Figure 17?

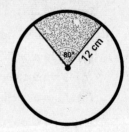

Fig. 17

9   Make a tally of the digits 0–9 as they appear in the value of π given on p. 48. Draw a bar chart to illustrate the result and comment upon it.

Interlude

SPROUTS

This is a game for two players.
Mark three dots anywhere on a sheet of paper (see Figure 1).

Fig. 1

Each player in turn draws a line joining a dot either to itself or to another dot and places a new dot on this line. Some possible opening moves are shown in Figure 2.

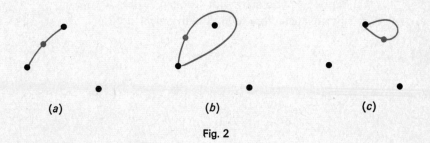

(a)   (b)   (c)

Fig. 2

No line may cross either itself or any other line and no dot may have more than three lines leaving it.

A typical game is shown in Figure 3. The moves of the first player are shown in red and those of the second player in black. The last player able to move wins the game.

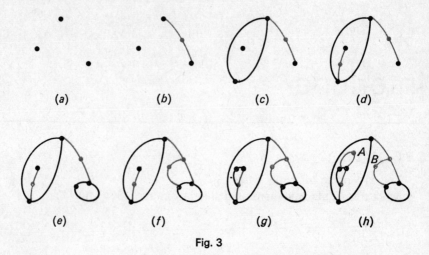

(a) (b) (c) (d)

(e) (f) (g) (h)

Fig. 3

A and *B* are the only dots which do not already have three lines leaving them and it is not possible to join *A* to *B* without crossing another line. So this game was won on the seventh move by 'red'.

Play several games with a friend; Sprouts is not as simple as it looks!

Look carefully at some finished games. Regard them as networks. How many arcs are there in each of the networks? How many nodes? What is the order of each of these nodes? Can you explain why a game of sprouts must end after at most 8 moves?

It is possible to vary the game by starting with 2 dots. After how many moves must the game now end?

What happens if you start with 4 dots or 5 dots or ...?

Why is it unsatisfactory to start with only 1 dot?

Revision exercises

Computation 1

1 $83.4 + 8.7$.

2 $250 - 12.4$.

3 78×2.3.

4 $3154 \div 38$.

5 $1\frac{1}{2} + \frac{3}{4} + \frac{5}{8}$.

6 $\begin{pmatrix} 0 & 1 \\ 2 & 3 \end{pmatrix} + \begin{pmatrix} -4 & 0 \\ 5 & -2 \end{pmatrix}$.

Computation 2

1 $19.3 + 18.4 - 17.5$.

2 $159.3 \div 2.7$.

3 Find the value of $15 \times$ sine of $65°$.

4 $(0.13)^2$.

5 $-4(5 - -3)$.

6 $\begin{pmatrix} 1 & 2 \\ 3 & 0 \end{pmatrix} \begin{pmatrix} 3 & -1 \\ 0 & 2 \end{pmatrix}$.

Slide Rule Session No. 1

In this exercise remember to find a rough answer first. Then use your slide rule to do the calculations. Try to give answers to 3 s.f. or to 2 s.f. depending on which end of the scale the answer comes.

1 3.2×1.7.

2 11.2×0.76.

3 $72 \div 3.4$.

4 $550 \div 0.17$.

5 $8 \times \pi \times 4.3$.

6 $(8.9)^2$.

7 $\dfrac{6.1 \times 21}{87}$.

8 $\dfrac{0.006 \times 29}{3.85}$.

9 $\sqrt{42}$.

10 $(74)^2 \times 0.325$.

Exercise A

1 What is 8% of £125?

2 $3(x+2) = 9$. Find the value of x.

3 What is the symmetry number of a cube?

4 (a) $1011_{\text{two}} + 11_{\text{two}}$; (b) $1011_{\text{two}} \times 11_{\text{two}}$. Give both answers in base two.

5 Write the following decimals as fractions in their simplest form:

(a) 0·8; (b) 0·84; (c) 0·822.

6 Write down the one-stage route matrix for the network in Figure 1.

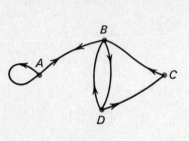

Fig. 1

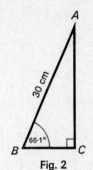

Fig. 2

7 Use your tables to help you find the lengths of AC and BC in Figure 2.

8 Onto what point is (⁻2, 3) mapped by the translation with vector $\begin{pmatrix} 4 \\ -1 \end{pmatrix}$?

Exercise B

1 $6_{\text{eight}} \times 7_{\text{eight}}$ in base eight.

2 Draw and give the names of two quadrilaterals which have only two lines of symmetry.

3 If $A = \{\text{prime numbers between 9 and 21}\}$ and $B = \{\text{odd numbers between 8 and 22}\}$, list the members of $A \cap B$.

4 Simplify

(a) $^{+}13 + ^{-}4$; (b) $^{-}11 + ^{-}6\frac{1}{2}$; (c) $^{-}8 - ^{-}9\frac{1}{2}$.

5 In Figure 3, $DC = 4$ cm and the area of triangle ABC is 16 cm². What is the length of AB?

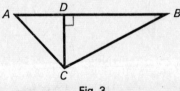

Fig. 3

6 Sketch, if possible, networks with

(a) one 4-node, one 3-node and one 1-node only;

(b) one 5-node, two 3-nodes and one 1-node only.

7 The area of a circle is increased from 16π cm² to 64π cm². What is the increase in the radius?

8 The answers to these calculations are either correct or *very* wrong. By making rough estimates, find out which are the wrong ones:

(a) $23 \cdot 1 \times 0 \cdot 22 = 49 \cdot 32$;   (b) $2300 \times 96 \cdot 7 = 220410$;

(c) $73 \cdot 472 \div 11 \cdot 2 = 6 \cdot 56$;   (d) $19 \cdot 7 \div 0 \cdot 41 = 8 \cdot 7$.

Exercise C (Multi-choice)

In this exercise there may be more than one correct answer to a question. Write down the letter (or letters) corresponding to the correct answer (or answers). Show any rough working that you do.

1 If $a = {}^-2, b = {}^-1, c = 1$, the value of $a^2(b-c)$ is

(a) 8;   (b) 0;   (c) ⁻8;   (d) none of these.

2 If the bearing of X from Y is 080° then the bearing of Y from X is:

(a) 100°;   (b) 260°;   (c) 080°;   (d) none of these.

3 Figure 4 shows a regular octahedron *ABCDEF*. Which of the following statements are true?

(a) The solid has exactly eight faces, six vertices and eight edges.

(b) The solid has just four planes of symmetry.

(c) $BF = ED$.

(d) The solid has just thirteen axes of symmetry.

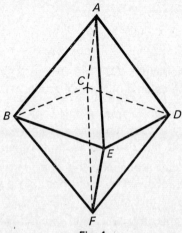

Fig. 4

4 A rectangle is enlarged by a factor of 2 and then the new rectangle is enlarged by a factor of ‾2. The resultant scale factor of the two enlargements is:

(a) 0;   (b) 4;   (c) ‾4;   (d) none of these.

5 123_{five} is

(a) prime;   (b) even;   (c) odd;   (d) a multiple of 34_{five}.

6 If the approximation to an unknown number is 4·6, to 2 significant figures, then the unknown number could be

(a) 4·54;   (b) 4·62;   (c) 4·58;   (d) 4·66.

Exercise D

1 A boy draws a straight chalk line 8 m long and then walks all the way round it so that he is always exactly 3 m from the line. Using a scale of 1 cm to 1 m, make an accurate drawing of the line and the boy's path.

2 Figure 5 shows the roof of a house (not drawn to scale). Use your slide rule and trigonometry tables to find the width of the roof (AB).

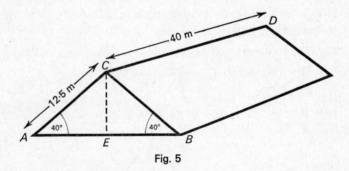

Fig. 5

Show that the height (CE) is 8·0 m to 2 s.f. Find the area of ABC and hence the volume of the roof space.

3 A girl draws marbles from a bag containing four green and six red marbles. She draws one marble at a time without looking and always returns it to the bag before drawing another.

(a) What is the probability that the first two draws result in (i) a green marble followed by a red one; (ii) a red marble followed by a green one?

(b) What is the probability that the first two draws result in (i) two marbles of the same colour; (ii) one marble of each colour?

4   A machine used in road repair work moves on a caterpillar track in the form of a band. The ends are semi-circles of radius 70 cm and are joined by two horizontal sections (see Figure 6). The complete length of the track is 800 cm. What length of the track rests on the road at any one time, that is, what is the length of *AB* ? (Take the value of π as $\frac{22}{7}$.)

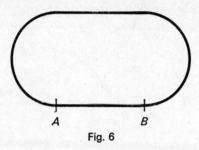

Fig. 6

5   Calculate the areas of the shapes in Figure 7.

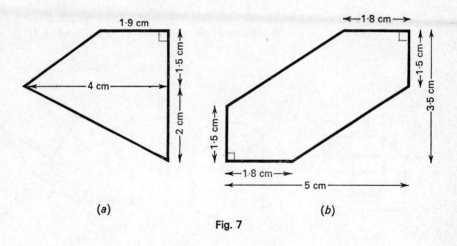

(a)   (b)

Fig. 7

6   A flagstaff is 15 m high and is held in position by ropes. One rope is fastened to a point 1 m below the top of the pole and is pegged at a distance of 5 m from its base, measured along level ground. What is the smallest number of complete metres of rope needed? (Neglect the lengths needed for tying, etc.)

Revision exercises

Exercise E

1 In Figure 8, *OB* is fixed, *OA* rotates around *O* and *AB* is a piece of elastic which is just less than 7 cm long when unstretched. *OA* = 5 cm and *OB* = 12 cm, and *M* is the mid-point of *AB*. Either set up the apparatus or use an accurate drawing to find the path traced out by *M* in one complete rotation of *OA*.

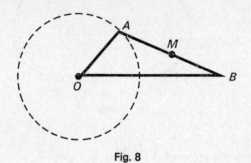

Fig. 8

2 Use your slide rule to calculate the volumes of the solids shown in Figure 9. (The cross-section of the prism in (*c*) is a rhombus.)

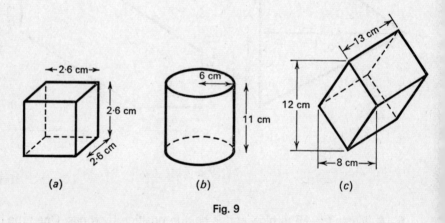

(*a*)   (*b*)   (*c*)

Fig. 9

3 A bag contains 4 lime, 5 orange and 6 lemon sweets. Anne takes a sweet without looking and eats it. Bill then does the same. What is the probability that

(*a*) they both pick a lime sweet;

(*b*) they both pick an orange sweet;

(*c*) Anne picks an orange sweet and Bill a lemon or lime one?

4   A cotton reel has 99 m of cotton wound round it. The reel is 3·5 cm in diameter. What is the circumference of the reel?

Use this to find the approximate number of times the reel will turn on a sewing machine before all the cotton is used up. Why will your calculated answer be different from the actual number of turns? Would you expect the reel to turn more times or less times before it is empty?

5   The right-angled triangle in Figure 10 is enlarged with centre O and scale factor 3 to give triangle OA_1B_1. What is

(*a*)   the length of AB;

(*b*)   the length of A_1B_1;

(*c*)   the area of triangle OA_1B_1?

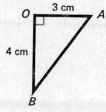

Fig. 10

6   Triangle ABC has vertices $A(1, 1)$, $B(3, 4)$ and $C(4, 2)$. Draw triangle ABC on squared paper.

(*a*)   Write down a 2 by 3 matrix to show the journeys from the origin to A, B and C.

(*b*)   Multiply this matrix by $\begin{pmatrix} 0 & -1 \\ -1 & 0 \end{pmatrix}$ on the left.

(*c*)   On your diagram show the image of ABC after the transformation represented by $\begin{pmatrix} 0 & -1 \\ -1 & 0 \end{pmatrix}$.

(*d*)   What transformation does $\begin{pmatrix} 0 & -1 \\ -1 & 0 \end{pmatrix}$ represent?

(*e*)   If $\mathbf{A} = \begin{pmatrix} 0 & -1 \\ -1 & 0 \end{pmatrix}$, describe the transformations represented by $\mathbf{A}^2$, $\mathbf{A}^3$ and $\mathbf{A}^4$.

5. Shearing

1. INVESTIGATIONS

For this work you will need about 12 to 15 used matchsticks. Colour one matchstick red with a felt-tip pen.

Investigation 1

Arrange the matchsticks in a rectangle with the red one as the base. Keep the red one fixed and use a ruler to help alter the shape as in Figure 1.

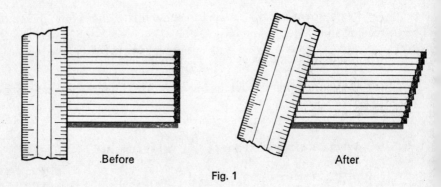

.Before   After

Fig. 1

What does the new shape look like?
Has the length of the base changed?
Has the height changed?
Has the area changed?

See what other shapes you can make, still starting with a rectangle and keeping the red match fixed. Comment upon what you find.

You should find that, however much you try, you can only make shapes which are like parallelograms (see Figure 2). In each case, the area of the parallelogram is equal to the area of the rectangle.

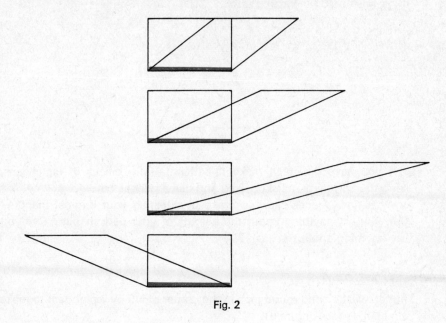

Fig. 2

This transformation is called a *shear*.

Investigation 2

Place the rectangle of matchsticks on a sheet of plain paper and draw round the outline. Keep the bottom matchstick fixed and use a ruler to help shear the rectangle. Draw round the new outline. See Figure 3.

Next, keep the top matchstick of the new figure fixed and shear again as in Figure 4 to make a rectangle. Draw round the outline.

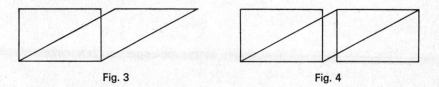

Fig. 3   Fig. 4

What single transformation has taken place?

How could you use shears to move the rectangle further across the page? (Remember that you must keep one matchstick fixed during a shear.)

Investigation 3

Draw a triangle like the one in Figure 5 and then draw a shape which you think this could be sheared into.

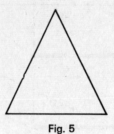

Fig. 5

If you have difficulty, make the triangle with pieces of matchstick, keep the bottom matchstick fixed and use a ruler as before.

What new shapes can you make by shearing your original triangle? Can you say anything about the heights of your new shapes? Can you say anything about the areas?

Investigation 4

Put an elastic band round pins in the corner of a 5 by 5 pinboard to make a rectangle (see Figure 6).

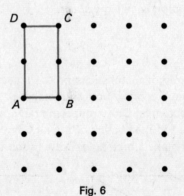

Fig. 6

Find how many different shears of this rectangle you can make:

   (*a*) keeping *AB* fixed;

   (*b*) keeping *DC* fixed;

   (*c*) keeping *CB* fixed;

   (*d*) keeping *AD* fixed.

What can you say about the areas of all the shapes you make?

Investigation 5

Make the following triangle on a 5 by 5 pinboard:

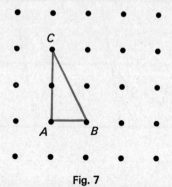

Fig. 7

Find how many different shears of triangle *ABC* you can make:

(*a*) keeping *AB* fixed;

(*b*) keeping *AC* fixed;

(*c*) keeping *BC* fixed.

What can you say about the areas of all the shapes you make?

Exercise A

1 Figure 8 shows a parallelogram before and after a translation. Copy the 'start' and 'finish' positions and show how to do the transformation with two shears. Why is it impossible to do it with one shear?

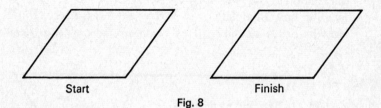

Start   Finish

Fig. 8

2 Copy Figure 9.

Show how you would go from *A* to *B* by the minimum number of shears.

Show how you would go from *A* to *C* by the minimum number of shears.

Can you go from *B* to *C* by shearing?

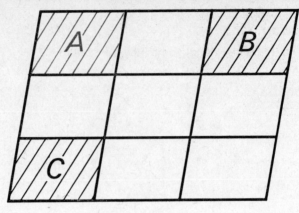

Fig. 9

3 Figure 10 shows a black triangle which has been sheared into a red triangle. Make a copy and put in three or four more possible shears of the black triangle, keeping *AB* fixed.

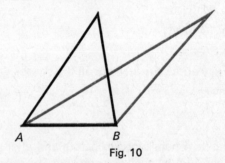

Fig. 10

4 The black parallelogram in Figure 11 has been sheared into the red parallelogram and *AR* = *RQ* = *QP* = *PB*.

How far has *Q* moved?   How far has *R* moved?

How far has *A* moved?   Which point on *AB* has not moved?

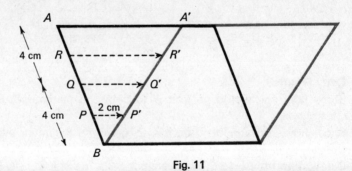

Fig. 11

5   Explain the difference between shearing a rectangle made of match-sticks and altering the shape of a hinged framework (see Figure 12).

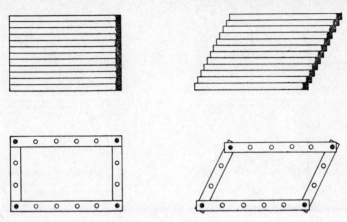

Fig. 12

2. PROPERTIES OF A SHEAR

2.1 The fixed line

For this section you will need your matchsticks again.

(*a*) Arrange the matchsticks in a rectangle as before, but this time put the red match in the middle (see Figure 13). What happens when you try to shear with a ruler keeping the red line fixed? What do you suggest you ought to do if you want to end up with a parallelogram?

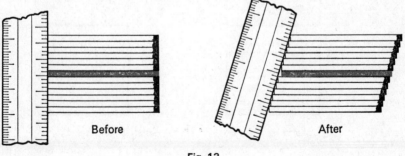

Before   After

Fig. 13

In which direction do the matches above the red line move? In which direction do the matches below the red line move?

Experiment by shearing other rectangles and placing the red match in different positions.

(*b*) Form the rectangle again, but this time do not use the red matchstick in the figure at all. Place it beneath as in Figure 14, keep it fixed and shear with the aid of a ruler.

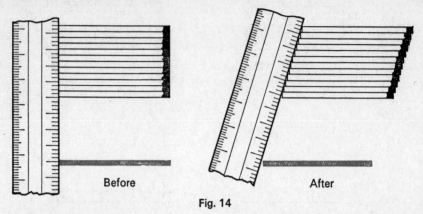

Before   After

Fig. 14

These two examples should help to show you that the fixed line of a shear does not have to be the base, or even a side. It can be any line inside or even outside the figure.

The line which remains unchanged by the shear is called the *invariant* line.

Exercise B

Copy the following figures and draw two or three possible shears of each, taking the red line as invariant in each case.

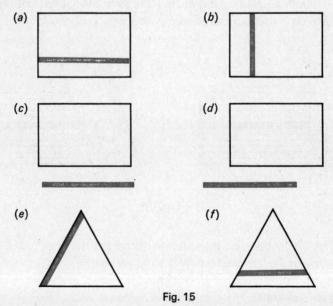

(*a*)   (*b*)

(*c*)   (*d*)

(*e*)   (*f*)

Fig. 15

(g)   (h)

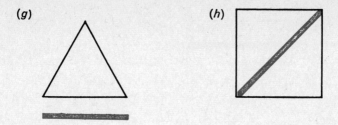

Fig. 15 (*cont.*)

2.2 Constructions

If we know the invariant line and the image of one point not on that line, then we can find the complete image under the shear transformation.

On a copy of Figure 16, take the red line as invariant and A' as the image of A and draw the complete image of the original figure. Is this the only possible solution?

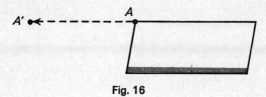

Fig. 16

Summary

A shear is a transformation in which:

(*a*) Area does not change.

(*b*) The points of a certain line are invariant.

(*c*) All other points move parallel to the invariant line.

(*d*) The ratio of the distance moved by points to their distance from the invariant line is constant.

Exercise C

1 Copy Figure 17. For each part, a point and its image are given. Taking the red line as invariant in each case, draw the transformed figure.

(*a*)

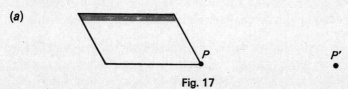

Fig. 17

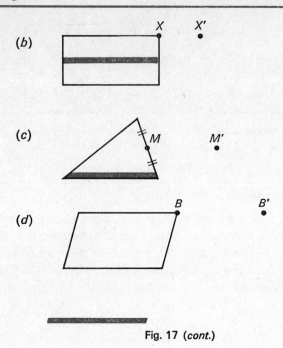

Fig. 17 (*cont.*)

2 Copy the triangle in Figure 18 and show how it can be sheared into:
  (*a*) an isosceles triangle;
  (*b*) a right-angled triangle.

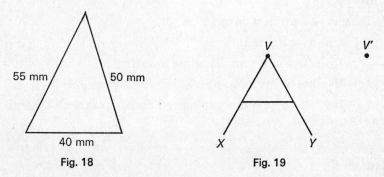

Fig. 18   Fig. 19

3 Draw the image of the letter *A* under the shear which has invariant line *XY* and maps *V* onto *V'* (see Figure 19).

4 Draw a diagram to show how a rectangle could be sheared to become another rectangle by using one diagonal as the invariant line.

5 A figure is sheared so that a point 2 cm from the invariant line moves 1 cm. How far does a point which is 4 cm from the invariant line move? Do the two points necessarily move in the same direction?

6. Trigonometry

1. A REMINDER

Here is a problem of a type you have met before:

A 10 m ladder leans against the wall of a house so that the angle between the ladder and the ground is 55°. How far up the wall does the ladder reach, and how far is the foot of the ladder from the wall?

Here are two ways of solving it:

First method

By scale drawing. See Figure 1.
Scale: 1 cm represents 2 m.

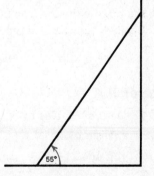

Fig. 1

The distance up the wall on the diagram is 4·1 cm, which represents 8·2 m.

Use your ruler to find how far the foot of the ladder is from the wall.

Second method

By using tables of sines and cosines.
Remember that:

the *x*-coordinate is given by the cosine,
the *y*-coordinate is given by the sine.

The information in Figure 2 (*a*) was obtained by looking up 55° in sine and cosine tables.

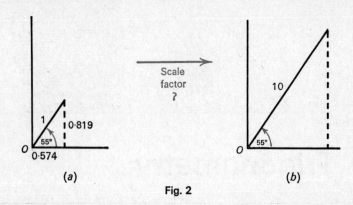

(*a*)   (*b*)

Fig. 2

What enlargement would map Figure 2 (*a*) onto Figure 2 (*b*)? Hence find the distances asked for in the question.

Check that the answers from the scale drawing method agree approximately with those obtained from the tables. Which method do you think is more reliable?

1.1 Abbreviations

We often write the sine of 55° as sin 55°.
Similarly, cosine is abbreviated to cos, for example,

$$\cos 55° = 0.574.$$

Exercise A

1   Use your tables to find the values of the following:

(*a*) sin 47·2°;   (*b*) 2 × sin 78·6°;

(*c*) cos 21·5°;   (*d*) 3 × cos 78·9°.

2   An aeroplane is climbing at an angle of 34° to the horizontal. Find its increase in height when it has gone 2000 m through the air, first by making an accurate scale drawing, and then by calculation using tables.

3 The jib of a crane is 30 m long and is inclined at 75° to the horizontal. Draw a rough sketch and then use tables to find how high the top of the jib is above its base.

4 A ship sails 68 km on a bearing of 032°. Draw a rough sketch.

What angle does its course make with the east–west direction?

How far north is it from its original position? How far east?

5 Find the scale factor which maps Figure 3 (*a*) onto Figure 3 (*b*). Hence find the size of the angle *a*.

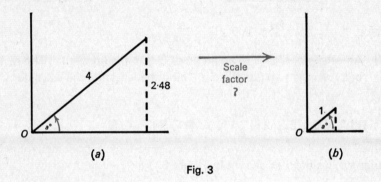

(*a*)   (*b*)

Fig. 3

6 Find the size of the angle *b* in Figure 4.

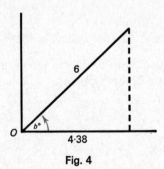

Fig. 4

7 A ladder 10 m long leans against a wall and the foot is 5·11 m from the wall. Find the angle of slope of the ladder, first by making a scale drawing, and then by calculation.

8 A mountain railway rises 92 m vertically in 400 m of track length. Use tables to find the angle of slope of the track.

9 Find the scale factor which maps Figure 5(*b*) onto Figure 5 (*a*). Hence find the length of *OP*.

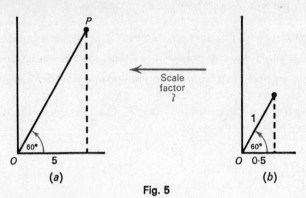

(*a*)   (*b*)

Fig. 5

10 An escalator slopes at an angle of 30° to the horizontal. The distance between the two floors is 6 m. Find the length of the escalator.

2. TRIANGLES IN ANY POSITION

In all the problems we have come across so far in trigonometry, the basic triangle has been as shown in Figure 6.

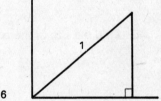

Fig. 6

We shall now deal with problems where the triangle is in a different position (see Figure 7, for example).

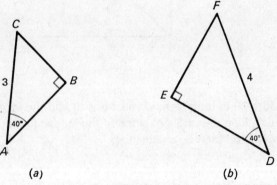

(*a*)   (*b*)

Fig. 7

(*a*) Figure 7 (*a*) can be transformed into the position shown in Figure 6 by a rotation. This is most easily done by rotating the book as shown in Figure 8.

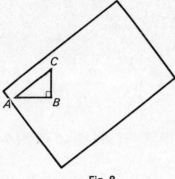

Fig. 8

It can be seen that the length of *AB* is

$$3 \times \cos 40° = 2·298.$$

What is the length of *BC*?

(*b*) In order to transform the triangle in Figure 7 (*b*) into the position shown in Figure 6 it has to be turned over. This can be done by a reflection, but it is easier to hold the page up to the light, and look through from the other side, rotating the book until *DE* is horizontal. Try it.

Then it can be seen that the length of *EF* is

$$4 \times \sin 40° = 2·572.$$

What is the length of *ED*?

Exercise B

Transform the triangles in Questions 1 and 2 to the position shown in Figure 6, and hence find the lengths and angles marked with letters.

1

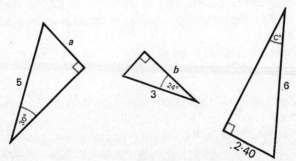

Fig. 9

2

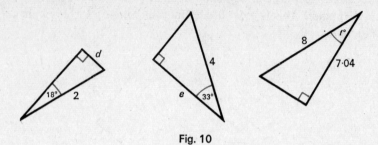

Fig. 10

3   Find the x- and y-coordinates of the points *A, B, C, D* in Figure 11.

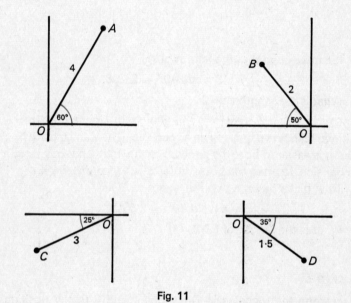

Fig. 11

4   A road slopes downwards at an angle of 12° to the horizontal for 3 km. Find the vertical distance descended in travelling along the road.

5   An aeroplane dives at an angle of 23° to the horizontal for 5 km. Find its change of height.

6   A pendulum of length 30 cm swings through 17° each side of the vertical (see Figure 12). When the pendulum bob is at the end of a swing, find how far it is below the point of suspension, that is, find the distance *PQ*. Hence find how far the pendulum bob rises from its bottom position.

Fig. 12

7 The ropes of a swing are 5 m long and they move through 40° each side of the vertical. At the lowest point of the swing, the seat is 0·5 m above the ground. How high is the point of suspension above the ground? What is the greatest height of the seat above the ground?

8 Figure 13 shows a section through a flower-pot. Calculate the diameter of the top of the pot. (*Hint*: use the red dotted lines.)

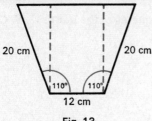

Fig. 13

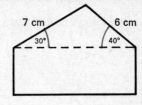

Fig. 14

9 Figure 14 shows a section of a barn. Calculate the width of the barn. (*Hint*: you will need to put in an extra line.)

10 The sloping sides of a V-shaped trough are 50 cm long. If the angle at the base of the trough is 40°, calculate the width across the top.

3. USING A SLIDE RULE

Most of the problems we have done so far have involved fairly easy numbers. Now we shall do some problems with more awkward numbers in them. You will find it best to use your slide rule.

In Figure 15, *OP* makes an angle of 35° with the line $y = 0$ and the length of *OP* is 7·3 units.

The *y*-coordinate of *P* is

$$7 \cdot 3 \times \sin 35°.$$

Use your tables and slide rule to work this out.

Calculate the *x*-coordinate of *P*.

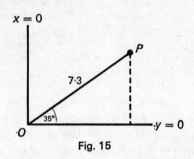

Fig. 15

Exercise C

1   Calculate the following: (*a*) $3 \cdot 2 \times \sin 16 \cdot 3°$; (*b*) $5 \cdot 2 \times \cos 83 \cdot 7°$; (*c*) $6 \cdot 8 \times \sin 63 \cdot 1°$.

2   In Figure 16, find the *x*-and *y*-coordinates of the points *A*, *B*, *C*.

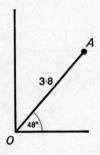

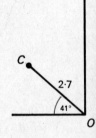

Fig. 16

3   In Figure 17, find the lengths indicated by letters.

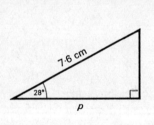
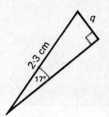
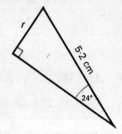

Fig. 17

4 A ladder of length 6·6 m leans against a wall at an angle of 37° to the horizontal. How far up the wall does it reach, and how far is the base of the ladder from the wall?

5 A ship sails 57·2 km on a bearing of 043°. What angle does its course make with the east-west line? How far north is it from its original position? How far east?

4. SCALE FACTORS

(a) What scale factor maps Figure 18 (a) onto Figure 18 (b)?

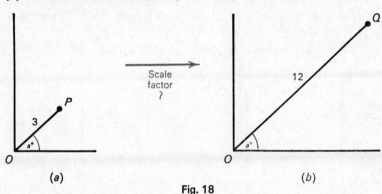

Fig. 18

To obtain your answer you had to divide 12 by 3.

Suppose OP was of length 7 and OQ of length 35. What would the scale factor be?

Copy and complete this table:

Length of OP	Length of OQ	Scale factor
2	6	
2	1	
3	15	
3	1	
5	30	

(b) You should have been able to work out the scale factors in your head. We shall now do some more difficult ones.

If the length of OP is 1·5, and the length of OQ is 6·6, then the scale factor is given by

$$6·6 \div 1·5.$$

You will find a slide rule useful to do this division. Check that you get 4·40.

Copy and complete this table:

Length of *OP*	Length of *OQ*	Scale factor
1·7	8·2	
0·64	8·2	
0·874	22·1	
8·42	1	

(*c*) In Figure 19, it is required to calculate the size of *b*.

OP has to be mapped onto *OP'*. This means that to map Figure 19(*a*) onto Figure 19(*b*) we must divide all lengths by 6·8. Hence find the *y*-coordinate of *P'*.

Look this up in your sine table and so find the value of *b*.

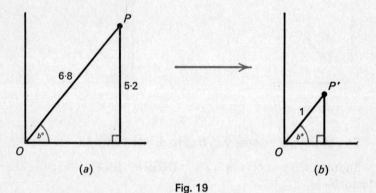

(*a*) (*b*)

Fig. 19

(*d*) In Figure 20(*a*), it is required to find the length indicated by the question mark.

The information in Figure 20(*b*) was obtained by looking up 25° in the cosine table.

What scale factor would map Figure 20(*b*) onto Figure 20(*a*)? Hence find the length indicated by the question mark.

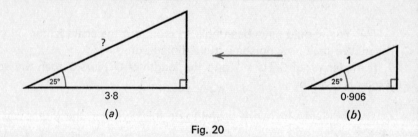

(*a*) (*b*)

Fig. 20

Exercise D

1   What must the lengths in Figure 21 (*a*) be divided by in order to map Figure 21 (*a*) onto Figure 21 (*b*) ? Hence find the value of *p*.

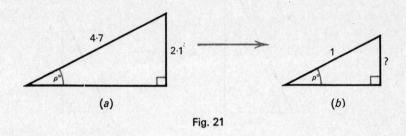

Fig. 21

2   What must the lengths in Figure 22 (*a*) be divided by in order to map Figure 22 (*a*) onto Figure 22 (*b*) ? Hence find the value of *q*.

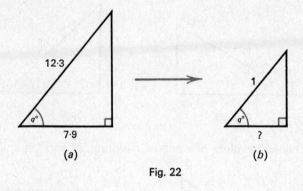

Fig. 22

3   First use tables to find the length indicated by the question mark in Figure 23 (*b*). Hence find the scale factor and the length *r*.

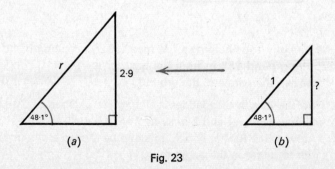

Fig. 23

87

4 First use tables to find the length indicated by the question mark in Figure 24 (*b*). Hence find the scale factor and the length *s*.

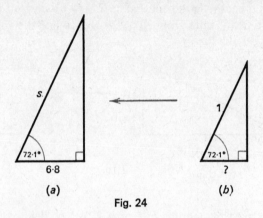

Fig. 24

5 Calculate the values of *t* and *u* in Figures 25 and 26.

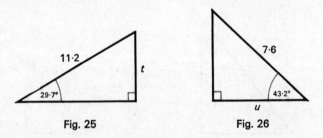

Fig. 25   Fig. 26

6 Calculate the values of *v* and *w* in Figures 27 and 28.

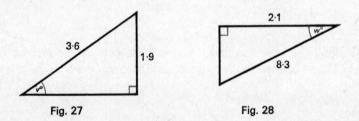

Fig. 27   Fig. 28

7 A wire guy-rope holding a T.V. mast is 190 m in length and is anchored to the ground 135 m from the base of the mast. Calculate the angle between the wire and the ground.

8 Find the length of a ladder which when inclined at 20° to a vertical wall has its lower end 2 m away from the wall.

How much further should this end be moved away from the wall in order to increase the angle to 30°?

9 Figure 29 shows two sections of a folding door. Find the size of the angle *BAC*.

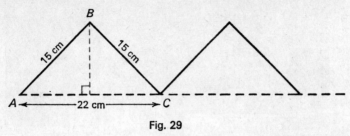

Fig. 29

10 A tunnel slopes downwards for 200 m at 30° to the horizontal and then upwards at 40° to the horizontal so that the two ends of the tunnel are at the same level. How long is the second part of the tunnel?

7. Formulas

1. WRITING DOWN FORMULAS

Formulas are useful in Mathematics and Science because they can present, in a neat form, information which might otherwise take a long sentence.

For example, if you want to explain how to find the circumference of a circle, you could just write

$$C = \pi d$$

instead of 'To find the circumference of a circle you multiply the diameter by π.'

The formula for finding the area of a circle is

$$A = \pi r^2.$$

Give this information in a sentence.

Did you remember that you must first square r and then multiply by π?

Exercise A

You might like to use a slide rule for some of the questions in this exercise.

1 To find the area of the rectangle in Figure 1 multiply the length by the width. Write this information as a formula.

Fig. 1   Fig. 2

2 (a) Write down a formula for the area of the square in Figure 2.

(b) Write down a formula for the perimeter of this square.

3 The perimeter of the rectangle in Figure 3 could be found from either of these formulas:
$$P = 2\ell + 2w$$
or
$$P = 2(\ell + w).$$

(a) Describe in your own words what each formula means.

(b) By using the values $\ell = 5$ cm and $w = 4$ cm, check that both formulas give the same answer.

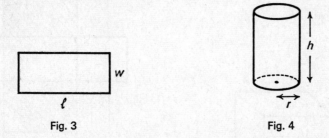

Fig. 3   Fig. 4

4 The volume of the cylinder in Figure 4 is obtained by multiplying the area of the base by the height. Complete the next two formulas. (*A* represents the area of the base and *V* represents the volume of the cylinder.)
$$A = \quad .$$
$$V = \quad .$$

5   The volume of the box in Figure 5 is given by $V = s \times s \times s$.

   (*a*) Write the formula for the volume more neatly.

   (*b*) Write down the volume if $s = 2$ cm. (It is *not* 6 cm³.)

   (*c*) What is the volume of the box if $s = 2 \cdot 3$ cm?

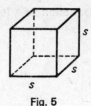

Fig. 5

6   (*a*) Complete this formula for the area of one face of the cube in Question 5:

$$A = \quad .$$

   (*b*) Explain how to find the total surface area of the six faces of the cube.

   (*c*) Write this as a formula if the total surface area is T:

$$T = \quad .$$

   (*d*) What is the total surface area of the cube if $s = 2 \cdot 3$ cm?

7   The volume of the box in Figure 6 is given by $V = \ell wh$.

   (*a*) Describe in your own words how to find the volume of the box.

   (*b*) Find the volume of the box if $\ell = 3 \cdot 4$ cm, $w = 3 \cdot 1$ cm and $h = 2 \cdot 6$ cm.

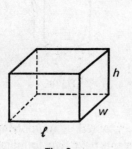

Fig. 6

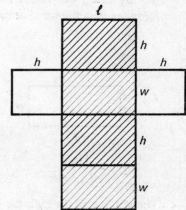

Fig. 7

8   (*a*) Figure 7 shows the net for a box of length ℓ, width w and height h.

      (i)   The area of card needed to make one of the faces shaded black is ℓh. So the area needed to make both of these faces is $2\ell h$.

(ii) What is the area of card needed to make the two faces shaded red?

(iii) What is the area of card needed to make the two faces which are unshaded?

(b) Call the total area of card needed to make the box A and copy and complete this expression for A:

$$A = 2\ell h + \quad + \quad .$$

(c) Put the values $\ell = 6$ cm, $w = 3\cdot5$ cm and $h = 4$ cm into the formula and work out the value of A.

2. FORMULAS FOR SOLVING PRACTICAL PROBLEMS

2.1 Working out the formulas

In *Book F*, Chapter 11, you solved some problems by drawing graphs. It was first necessary to write information as formulas.

Here is a problem like one you met there:

Jane went to a fair and wanted to have a number of rides on the dodgems, which cost 5 pence a ride, and the rockets, which cost 6 pence a ride.

Write an expression to show how much it would cost her to have d rides on the dodgems and r rides on the rockets.

Each dodgem ride costs 5 pence, so

2 dodgem rides would cost $2 \times 5 = 10$ pence,
4 dodgem rides would cost $4 \times 5 = 20$ pence,
d dogdem rides would cost $d \times 5 = 5d$ pence.

Each rocket ride costs 6 pence, so

2 rocket rides would cost $2 \times 6 = 12$ pence,
4 rocket rides would cost $4 \times 6 = 24$ pence,
r rocket rides would cost $r \times 6 = 6r$ pence.

The total cost of d dodgem rides and r rocket rides would be

$$(5d + 6r) \text{ pence.}$$

Exercise B

1 For a particular train journey the First Class fare is £3 and the Second Class fare is £2.

(a) Write an expression for the total money taken from F First Class passengers and S Second Class passengers.

(b) How much money would be taken if $F = 50$ and $S = 140$?

2 A town has single decker buses which can carry 40 passengers each and double decker buses which can carry 60 passengers each.

(*a*) How many passengers could be carried in *s* single decker buses and *d* double decker buses?

(*b*) If *s* = 50 and *d* = 30, how many passengers could be carried?

(*c*) What is the total number of buses being used in part (*b*)?

3 In a flower shop, daffodils cost 12 pence a bunch and tulips cost 15 pence a bunch.

(*a*) What would be the cost of *d* bunches of daffodils and *t* bunches of tulips?

(*b*) How much would the shop take if one day it sold 24 bunches of daffodils and 18 bunches of tulips?

4 For a School Play, reserved seats cost 25 pence each and unreserved seats cost 15 pence each.

(*a*) How much money would be taken from *r* reserved seats and *u* unreserved seats?

(*b*) If on one night, *r* = 100 and *u* = 80, how many seats were sold and how much money was taken?

5 In the game of battleships, a destroyer takes up one square, a warship 2 squares and an aircraft carrier 3 squares.

What is the total number of squares taken up by *d* destroyers, *w* warships and *a* aircraft carriers?

2.2 Getting information from formulas

In the example at the beginning of Section 2.1 we found that the total cost of *d* dodgem rides and *r* rocket rides was

$$(5d + 6r) \text{ pence.}$$

If Jane wanted to spend *exactly* 30 pence, how could she do it?
We want to find values of *d* and *r* so that

$$5d + 6r = 30.$$

She cannot have half rides, so we need only worry about whole numbers.

When *d* is 0, $6r = 30$ and so $r = 5$.
She could have no dodgem rides and 5 rocket rides.

When *d* is 1, $6r = 25$ and so $r = 4\frac{1}{6}$, which is not possible.

When *d* is 2, $6r = 20$ and so $r = 3\frac{1}{3}$. Is this possible?

Continue in this way to find other possible values.
What happens when *d* is 7? Is it worth trying any larger values of *d*?

Exercise C

1 In a game, drawing out a red counter scores 2 points and drawing out a blue counter scores 1 point. Peter has scored 12 points. How could he have done this? To score 12 points:

$$2r + b = 12.$$

If $r = 0$, $b = 12$. He could have 0 red and 12 blue counters.
If $r = 1$, $b = 10$. He could have 1 red and 10 blue counters.
You might prefer to write your results in a table like this:

r	b
0	12
1	10
.	.
.	.

Continue to find all the other possible combinations.

2 The game in Question 1 is now changed so that a red counter scores 3 points and a blue counter 2 points.

(*a*) Copy and complete the following relation which must be true if you score 12 points:

$$3r + \quad b = 12.$$

(*b*) Find all the possible values for r and b which give a score of 12. (Remember you cannot take parts of a counter!)

3 $2r + 5b = 40$.

(*a*) What is b when r is 5?

(*b*) What is r when b is 4?

(*c*) Are there any other possible whole number (or zero) values for r and b? If so, find them.

(*d*) If this formula referred to a game like the one in Questions 1 and 2, how many points would each red counter score?

4 A girl went into a flower shop with 60 pence to spend on violets at 10 pence a bunch and primroses at 6 pence a bunch.

(*a*) If she is to spend all her money on v bunches of violets and p bunches of primroses, copy and complete the expression:

$$10v + 6p = \quad .$$

(*b*) Work out all the possible ways in which she can do this. Half bunches are not allowed!

5   A town has *s* single decker buses which take 40 people each and *d* double decker buses which take 60 people each.

(*a*) Write down an expression which must be true if the town wants bus spaces to carry 1200 passengers.

(*b*) If *s* is 0, what is *d*?

(*c*) If *d* is 0, what is *s*?

(*d*) If *s* is 15, what is *d*?

(*e*) Can you find any other whole number values for *s* and *d*?

(*f*) Write a sentence to describe the various ways in which the town can decide to buy its buses.

3. SCIENTIFIC FORMULAS

You may have used some formulas in Science lessons.

(*a*) Here is one you may have encountered in your work on electricity:
$$W = IV.$$
W stands for the power in a circuit, I for the current and V for the voltage.

If you are told that $I = 0{\cdot}5$ and $V = 240$, what is W?

(*b*) Let us look again at
$$W = IV.$$
If you know that $W = 60$ and $V = 240$, what is I?

To find the value of I, put the values you know into the formula:
$$60 = I \times 240.$$
Can you now say what I is?

Sometimes the arithmetic is not so easy and you cannot spot the answer quickly.

(*c*) Suppose you have
$$v = u + at,$$
and you know that $v = 44$, $u = 4$, and $a = 5$. What is t?

To find t, put the values you know in the formula:
$$44 = 4 + 5t.$$
Perhaps you can spot the value of t. If not, work it out by completing this flow diagram:

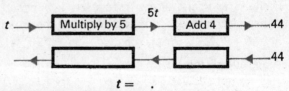

$$t = \quad .$$

96

Exercise D

1 $F = ma$.
   (a) What is m if $F = 80$ and $a = 20$?
   (b) What is a if $F = 60$ and $m = 7 \cdot 5$?

2 $d = \dfrac{v^2}{20}$.
   (a) Find d when v is 40. (b) Find v when d is 45.

3 Here is another Physics formula:
$$PV = RT.$$
   If $P = 8$, $V = 5$ and $R = 4$, what is T?

4 $v = u + at$.
   (a) If $u = 10$, $a = 6$ and $t = 2 \cdot 5$, what is v?
   (b) If $v = 20$, $a = 8$ and $t = 1 \cdot 5$, what is u?
   (c) If $v = 30$, $u = 22$ and $a = 4$, what is t?

5 $F = \dfrac{mv^2}{R}$. (This means that to find F you must first square v, then multiply by m and divide by R.)
   (a) If $m = 8$, $v = 3$ and $R = 6$, what is F?
   (b) If $F = 18$, $m = 6$ and $v = 3$, what is R?

6 $E = \frac{1}{2}mv^2$.
   (a) Find E if $m = 10$ and $v = 5$.
   (b) Find m if $E = 18$ and $v = 3$.
   (c) Find v if $E = 56$ and $m = 7$.

7 $F = \dfrac{mv - mu}{t}$.
   (a) Find F if $m = 10$, $v = 6$, $u = 4$ and $t = 2$.
   (b) Find t if $m = 8$, $v = 5$, $u = 3$ and $F = 2$.
   (c) Find u if $m = 12$, $v = 8$, $t = 9$ and $F = 4$.

8 In work on lenses or mirrors you may have met the formula
$$\frac{1}{u} + \frac{1}{v} = \frac{1}{f}.$$
   (a) If $u = 6$ and $v = 3$, what is f? (f is *not* 9.)
   (b) If $u = 4$ and $f = 2$, what is $\dfrac{1}{v}$? What is v?
   (c) If $v = 6$ and $f = 2$, what is u?

8. Matrices and transformations

1. TRANSFORMATIONS

(a) The matrix

$$\begin{array}{cccc} A & B & C & D \end{array}$$
$$\begin{pmatrix} ^-1 & 1 & 1 & ^-3 \\ 2 & 1 & ^-1 & ^-1 \end{pmatrix}$$

shows the journeys from the origin to the vertices of the quadrilateral in Figure 1.

Multiply this matrix by the matrix $\begin{pmatrix} 2 & 0 \\ 0 & 2 \end{pmatrix}$ on the left, that is, work out

$$\begin{pmatrix} 2 & 0 \\ 0 & 2 \end{pmatrix}\begin{array}{cccc} A & B & C & D \\ \begin{pmatrix} ^-1 & 1 & 1 & ^-3 \\ 2 & 1 & ^-1 & ^-1 \end{pmatrix} \end{array} = \begin{array}{cccc} A_1 & B_1 & C_1 & D_1 \\ \begin{pmatrix} & & & \end{pmatrix} \end{array}.$$

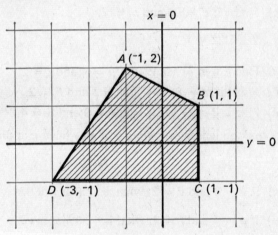

Fig. 1

On a diagram show the quadrilateral $ABCD$ and its image $A_1B_1C_1D_1$ after the transformation represented by $\begin{pmatrix} 2 & 0 \\ 0 & 2 \end{pmatrix}$.

Describe the transformation as accurately as you can.

What happens to:

    (i)   lengths of lines,

    (ii) areas of shapes,

    (iii) angles?

(b) Write down the 2 by 4 matrix which shows the journeys from the origin to the vertices of the rectangle in Figure 2.

Multiply this matrix by the matrix $\begin{pmatrix} 2 & 0 \\ 0 & 1 \end{pmatrix}$ on the left to find the journeys from the origin to P_1, Q_1, R_1 and S_1. Draw the rectangle and its image.

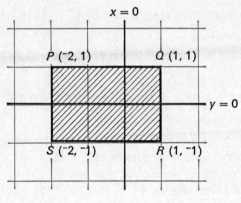

Fig. 2

Now draw diagrams to show the effect of the matrix $\begin{pmatrix} 2 & 0 \\ 0 & 1 \end{pmatrix}$ on each of the shapes shown in Figure 3.

What happens to:

    (i)   lengths of lines parallel to $x = 0$,

    (ii) lengths of lines parallel to $y = 0$,

    (iii) areas of shapes,

    (iv) points which lie on the line $x = 0$,

    (v) points which lie on the line $y = 0$?

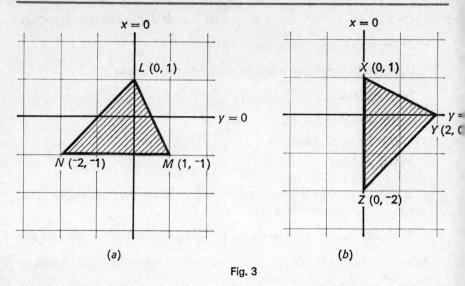

Fig. 3

The transformation represented by $\begin{pmatrix} 2 & 0 \\ 0 & 1 \end{pmatrix}$ is called a *one-way stretch*. Can you see why?

Each shape is 'stretched' from the line $x = 0$ with stretch factor 2.

(c) Draw diagrams to show the effect of the matrix $\begin{pmatrix} 1 & 0 \\ 0 & 3 \end{pmatrix}$ on each of the shapes shown in Figures 2 and 3.

What happens this time to:

(i) lengths of lines parallel to $x = 0$,
(ii) lengths of lines parallel to $y = 0$,
(iii) areas of shapes,
(iv) points which lie on the line $x = 0$,
(v) points which lie on the line $y = 0$?

Describe the transformation as accurately as you can.

Exercise A

1 Write down the 2 by 4 matrix which shows the journeys from the origin to the vertices of the parallelogram in Figure 4.

Multiply this matrix by the matrix $\begin{pmatrix} 2 & 1 \\ 1 & 2 \end{pmatrix}$ on the left to find the journeys from the origin to A_1, B_1, C_1 and D_1.

Draw the parallelogram and its image.

What is the shape of $A_1 B_1 C_1 D_1$?

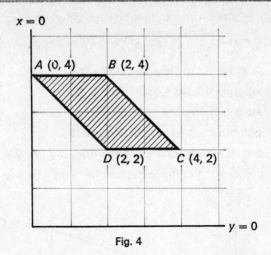

Fig. 4

2 Draw a diagram to show the effect of the matrix $\begin{pmatrix} 3 & 0 \\ 0 & 1 \end{pmatrix}$ on the square in Figure 5. Describe the transformation which this matrix represents.

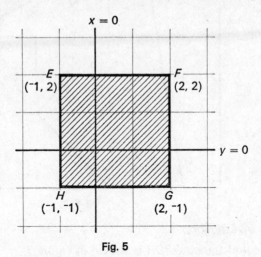

Fig. 5

3 Draw a diagram to show the effect of the matrix $\begin{pmatrix} -3 & 0 \\ 0 & -3 \end{pmatrix}$ on the square in Figure 5. Describe the transformation which this matrix represents.

4 Draw diagrams to show the effect of each of the following matrices on some shapes of your own choice.

(a) $\begin{pmatrix} -1 & 0 \\ 0 & -1 \end{pmatrix}$;   (b) $\begin{pmatrix} 0 & 1 \\ 1 & 0 \end{pmatrix}$;   (c) $\begin{pmatrix} 1 & 0 \\ 0 & \frac{1}{2} \end{pmatrix}$.

What transformation does each of these matrices represent?

5 Copy Figure 6 onto squared paper. On your diagram show the effect of the matrix $\begin{pmatrix} 1 & 1 \\ 0 & 1 \end{pmatrix}$ on Mr Poly. What happens to:

(a) lengths of lines parallel to $y = 0$;

(b) lengths of lines parallel to $x = 0$;

(c) area;

(d) points which lie on the line $y = 0$;

(e) points which are 3 cm away from the line $y = 0$;

(f) points which are 6 cm away from the line $y = 0$?

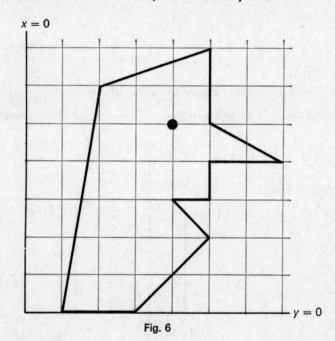

Fig. 6

6 *An investigation*

The unit square *OPQR* is shown in Figure 7.

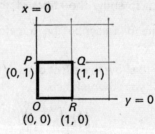

Fig. 7

Investigate the effect on the unit square of each of the following matrices.

(a) $\begin{pmatrix} 1 & 2 \\ 0 & 1 \end{pmatrix}$;   (b) $\begin{pmatrix} 1 & 3 \\ 0 & 1 \end{pmatrix}$;   (c) $\begin{pmatrix} 1 & \frac{1}{2} \\ 0 & 1 \end{pmatrix}$;   (d) $\begin{pmatrix} 1 & -1 \\ 0 & 1 \end{pmatrix}$;

(e) $\begin{pmatrix} 1 & 0 \\ 2 & 1 \end{pmatrix}$;   (f) $\begin{pmatrix} 1 & 0 \\ 3 & 1 \end{pmatrix}$;   (g) $\begin{pmatrix} 1 & 0 \\ \frac{1}{2} & 1 \end{pmatrix}$;   (h) $\begin{pmatrix} 1 & 0 \\ -2 & 1 \end{pmatrix}$.

Where have you met this type of transformation before?

Describe as accurately as you can the transformation which each matrix represents.

2. INVERSE TRANSFORMATIONS

(a) Draw a diagram to show the effect of the matrix $\begin{pmatrix} 1 & 0 \\ 0 & 1 \end{pmatrix}$ on some shape of your own choice.

What is special about the effect of this matrix? What transformation does it represent?

(b) Draw a diagram to show the effect of the matrix $\begin{pmatrix} 1 & 0 \\ 0 & -1 \end{pmatrix}$ on the triangle in Figure 8.

What transformation does this matrix represent?

What is the inverse of this transformation, that is, what transformation would map the final triangle back to its original position?

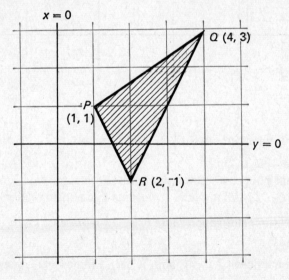

Fig. 8

We say that reflection in the line $y = 0$ is a self-inverse transformation.

Work out

$$\begin{pmatrix} 1 & 0 \\ 0 & -1 \end{pmatrix}\begin{pmatrix} 1 & 0 \\ 0 & -1 \end{pmatrix}.$$

Is $\begin{pmatrix} 1 & 0 \\ 0 & -1 \end{pmatrix}$ a self-inverse matrix for the operation of multiplication?

(c) Draw a diagram to show the rectangle in Figure 9 and its image $A_1B_1C_1D_1$ after the transformation represented by the matrix $\begin{pmatrix} 0 & -1 \\ 1 & 0 \end{pmatrix}$.
Describe this transformation.
What is the inverse of this transformation?

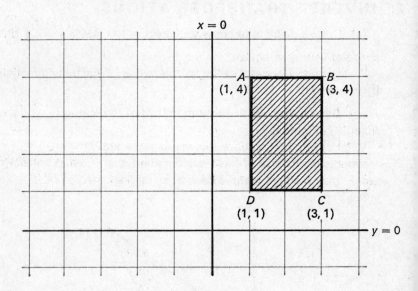

Fig. 9

Now transform $A_1B_1C_1D_1$ by the matrix $\begin{pmatrix} 0 & 1 \\ -1 & 0 \end{pmatrix}$ and label the new image $A_2B_2C_2D_2$.
What happens? What single transformation would map $ABCD$ onto $A_2B_2C_2D_2$? What matrix represents this transformation?
What transformation must $\begin{pmatrix} 0 & 1 \\ -1 & 0 \end{pmatrix}$ represent?

The matrices $\begin{pmatrix} 0 & -1 \\ 1 & 0 \end{pmatrix}$ and $\begin{pmatrix} 0 & 1 \\ -1 & 0 \end{pmatrix}$ represent inverse transformations.

Work out $\begin{pmatrix} 0 & -1 \\ 1 & 0 \end{pmatrix}\begin{pmatrix} 0 & 1 \\ -1 & 0 \end{pmatrix}$ and $\begin{pmatrix} 0 & 1 \\ -1 & 0 \end{pmatrix}\begin{pmatrix} 0 & -1 \\ 1 & 0 \end{pmatrix}.$

Is $\begin{pmatrix} 0 & 1 \\ -1 & 0 \end{pmatrix}$ the multiplicative inverse of $\begin{pmatrix} 0 & -1 \\ 1 & 0 \end{pmatrix}$?

What is the multiplicative inverse of $\begin{pmatrix} 0 & 1 \\ -1 & 0 \end{pmatrix}$?

Exercise B

1 (a) Draw a diagram to show the effect of the matrix $\begin{pmatrix} -1 & 0 \\ 0 & -1 \end{pmatrix}$ on the triangle in Figure 8.

(b) What transformation does $\begin{pmatrix} -1 & 0 \\ 0 & -1 \end{pmatrix}$ represent?

(c) What is the inverse of this transformation?

(d) What do you think is the multiplicative inverse of the matrix

$$\begin{pmatrix} -1 & 0 \\ 0 & -1 \end{pmatrix}?$$

(e) Check that $\begin{pmatrix} -1 & 0 \\ 0 & -1 \end{pmatrix}\begin{pmatrix} -1 & 0 \\ 0 & -1 \end{pmatrix} = \begin{pmatrix} 1 & 0 \\ 0 & 1 \end{pmatrix}$.

2 (a) Draw a diagram to show the effect of the matrix $\begin{pmatrix} 0 & -1 \\ -1 & 0 \end{pmatrix}$ on the rectangle in Figure 9.

(b) What transformation does $\begin{pmatrix} 0 & -1 \\ -1 & 0 \end{pmatrix}$ represent?

(c) What is the inverse of this transformation?

(d) What is the multiplicative inverse of the matrix $\begin{pmatrix} 0 & -1 \\ -1 & 0 \end{pmatrix}$?

3 Transform the rectangle in Figure 9 by the matrix $\begin{pmatrix} 1 & 1 \\ 0 & 1 \end{pmatrix}$.
Label the image $A_1B_1C_1D_1$.
Now transform $A_1B_1C_1D_1$ by the matrix $\begin{pmatrix} 1 & -1 \\ 0 & 1 \end{pmatrix}$. Label the new image $A_2B_2C_2D_2$. What happens?
What can you say about the matrices $\begin{pmatrix} 1 & 1 \\ 0 & 1 \end{pmatrix}$ and $\begin{pmatrix} 1 & -1 \\ 0 & 1 \end{pmatrix}$?

4   Start with a shape of your own choice. Transform it by the matrix $\begin{pmatrix} 3 & 2 \\ 1 & 1 \end{pmatrix}$ and then transform the new shape by the matrix $\begin{pmatrix} 1 & -2 \\ -1 & 3 \end{pmatrix}$.

What single transformation maps the original shape onto the final shape?

What matrix represents this transformation?

What is the multiplicative inverse of the matrix $\begin{pmatrix} 3 & 2 \\ 1 & 1 \end{pmatrix}$?

5   The matrix $\begin{pmatrix} 2 & 0 \\ 0 & 2 \end{pmatrix}$ represents an enlargement centre the origin and scale factor 2. What transformations do you think the following matrices represent?

(a) $\begin{pmatrix} 3 & 0 \\ 0 & 3 \end{pmatrix}$;   (b) $\begin{pmatrix} \frac{1}{4} & 0 \\ 0 & \frac{1}{4} \end{pmatrix}$;   (c) $\begin{pmatrix} -\frac{1}{2} & 0 \\ 0 & -\frac{1}{2} \end{pmatrix}$.

In each case describe the inverse transformation and use it to write down the multiplicative inverse of the matrix.

6   The matrix $\begin{pmatrix} 2 & 0 \\ 0 & 1 \end{pmatrix}$ represents a one-way stretch from $x = 0$ with stretch factor 2. What transformations do you think the following matrices represent?

(a) $\begin{pmatrix} 3 & 0 \\ 0 & 1 \end{pmatrix}$;   (b) $\begin{pmatrix} \frac{1}{2} & 0 \\ 0 & 1 \end{pmatrix}$.

In each case describe the inverse transformation and use it to write down the multiplicative inverse of the matrix.

7   Describe the transformation which $\begin{pmatrix} 1 & 0 \\ 0 & \frac{1}{4} \end{pmatrix}$ represents.

What is the inverse transformation? Write down the matrix which represents the inverse transformation.

8   Draw a diagram to show the effect of the matrix $\begin{pmatrix} 1 & -2 \\ 0 & 1 \end{pmatrix}$ on the unit square. Describe the transformation which this matrix represents. Describe the inverse transformation and use it to write down the multiplicative inverse of the matrix $\begin{pmatrix} 1 & -2 \\ 0 & 1 \end{pmatrix}$.

3. MATRICES AND AREA: AN INVESTIGATION

Find the area of the square in Figure 10.

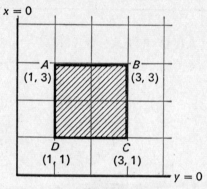

Fig. 10

Transform the square *ABCD* by each of the following matrices and by some others of your own choice.

(a) $\begin{pmatrix} 2 & 0 \\ 0 & 2 \end{pmatrix}$;   (b) $\begin{pmatrix} 1 & 0 \\ 0 & 3 \end{pmatrix}$;   (c) $\begin{pmatrix} 3 & 0 \\ 0 & 2 \end{pmatrix}$;   (d) $\begin{pmatrix} 3 & 0 \\ 1 & 1 \end{pmatrix}$;

(e) $\begin{pmatrix} 1 & 1 \\ 1 & 2 \end{pmatrix}$;   (f) $\begin{pmatrix} 1 & -1 \\ 1 & 1 \end{pmatrix}$;   (g) $\begin{pmatrix} 0 & -1 \\ 1 & 0 \end{pmatrix}$;   (h) $\begin{pmatrix} 1 & 2 \\ 1 & 4 \end{pmatrix}$.

Find the area of the new shape in each case and enter your results in a copy of the following table:

Original area	Transformation matrix	New area
4 cm²	$\begin{pmatrix} 2 & 0 \\ 0 & 2 \end{pmatrix}$	16 cm²
4 cm²	$\begin{pmatrix} 1 & 0 \\ 0 & 3 \end{pmatrix}$	12 cm²

There is a connection between the numbers in a transformation matrix and the effect it has on the area of a shape. See if you can spot this connection.

Does your answer work for the matrix $\begin{pmatrix} 4 & 1 \\ 3 & 2 \end{pmatrix}$? If not, try again.

Interlude

COUNTING AND MEASURING

We are going to look at the two questions, 'How many?' and 'How much?'

Greengrocer's scales

If you buy 1 kg of potatoes you can tell exactly how many potatoes you have just by counting them, but can you say that you have exactly 1 kg?

As far as the greengrocer is concerned, the potatoes weigh 1 kg, but if you took them home and weighed them on the kitchen scales you might find that they weigh 1·10 kg.

Kitchen scales

Laboratory balance

You might next take them to school and weigh them on a very accurate balance in the laboratory and find that they weigh 1·136 kg. An even more accurate method of weighing could be found in a specialised laboratory which might give the weight as 1·1358 kg.

What answer are you going to give to the following two questions?

> 'How many potatoes?'
> 'How much potato weight?'

How many pages has this book? How wide is it? Are these two questions equally easy to answer?

When we answer the questions 'How *many* potatoes?', 'How *many* pages?' we use the counting numbers 1, 2, 3, ... and our answer should always be exact.

When we try to answer the questions 'How *much* potato weight?' 'How *much* page width?', we have to measure and our answers will vary depending upon the instruments used to do the measuring.

You should now be able to see that these two questions are of a very different nature. When we are able to *count* the number of objects, we say we have a DISCRETE situation. When we have to *measure*, and can consequently only give an approximate answer, we say that we have a CONTINUOUS situation.

Here is a list of some of the statistical surveys you may have carried out in *Books B* and *C*. Consider each one and say whether the classifications and the results collected were continuous or discrete.

Title	Classification	Result collected
Travelling to school	Method of travel	Number of pupils
How the day is spent	Various activities	Time spent on each
The school week	Subjects on time-table	Time spent on each
A man's monthly expenditure	Items on which money was spent	Amount spent on each item
A vehicle survey	Types of vehicle	Number of each type
Letter frequency	Letters of the alphabet	Number of each letter
Size of family	Number of children per family	Number of families
Heights of class	Heights	Number of pupils
Ages of class	Ages	Number of pupils
Size of shoe	Shoe sizes	Number of pupils
Test results	Marks 0–10	Number of pupils

Discuss and criticise the following statements, saying how exact each one is:

(*a*) At the third stroke it will be three twenty-one precisely.

(*b*) School finishes at 4 o'clock.

(*c*) I live exactly 3 km from school.

(*d*) One lap of the athletics track is 500 metres.

(*e*) The train was 1 hour late.

(*f*) Net contents 50 matches.

(*g*) Take two eggs and $\frac{1}{4}$ kg of flour.

Revision exercises

Computation 3

1 $5 \cdot 33 + 55 \cdot 3$.

2 $71 \cdot 4 \div 17$.

3 Find the value of $26 \times \sin 50 \cdot 4°$.

4 $(7 + {}^-4 - {}^-6 + 5) \times 3$.

5 $\begin{pmatrix} {}^-1 & 0 \\ 5 & {}^-3 \end{pmatrix} + \begin{pmatrix} 2 & {}^-3 \\ {}^-4 & {}^-5 \end{pmatrix}$.

6 $2 \cdot 5 \%$ of £400.

Computation 4

1 $67 - 8 \cdot 8$.

2 $4170 \times 0 \cdot 82$.

3 Find the mean of 131, 133, 138, 142, 143, 147.

4 $\sqrt{(9 \times 16)}$.

5 $\begin{pmatrix} 3 & 1 \\ {}^-1 & 2 \end{pmatrix} \begin{pmatrix} 0 & {}^-1 \\ 1 & 4 \end{pmatrix}$.

6 $\frac{3}{7}$ of 826.

Slide Rule Session No. 2

1 $8 \cdot 4 \times 9 \cdot 1$.

2 $350 \times 0 \cdot 195$.

3 $0 \cdot 49 \div 2 \cdot 8$.

4 $77 \div 0 \cdot 45$.

5 $(8 \cdot 5)^2 \times \pi$.

6 $19 \times \sqrt{18}$.

7 $0 \cdot 61 \times 3 \cdot 2 \times 47$.

8 $(1 \cdot 7)^3$.

9 $3 \cdot 5 \times (1 \cdot 2)^3$.

10 $\dfrac{540 \times 1 \cdot 67}{23}$.

Exercise F

1 Convert 232_{four} to base ten.

2 Express $2 \cdot 6721$ (a) correct to 2 decimal places, (b) correct to 2 significant figures.

3 A circular brake disc has a radius of 12 cm. Calculate its area.

4 Draw a network described by the matrix

$$\begin{array}{c c} & \begin{array}{cccc} A & B & C & D \end{array} \\ \begin{array}{c} A \\ B \\ C \\ D \end{array} & \begin{pmatrix} 2 & 0 & 1 & 0 \\ 0 & 2 & 1 & 2 \\ 1 & 1 & 0 & 0 \\ 0 & 2 & 0 & 0 \end{pmatrix} \end{array}.$$

5 Find the lengths and angles marked with letters in Figure 1.

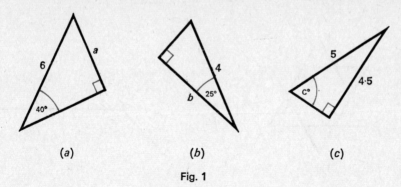

(a)   (b)   (c)

Fig. 1

6 The surface area, *A*, of a closed cylinder is given approximately by the formula

$$A = 6r(r+h).$$

(a) If *r* = 5 cm and *h* = 7 cm, what is *A*?

(b) If *A* = 180 cm² and *r* = 2 cm, what is *h*?

7 A box contains 36 marbles, some red and some blue. If a marble is drawn at random from the box, the probability that it is red is ¼. How many of the marbles are blue?

8 (a) Describe the transformation which $\begin{pmatrix} 1 & 0 \\ 0 & 3 \end{pmatrix}$ represents.

(b) What is the inverse transformation?

(c) Write down the matrix which represents this inverse transformation.

Exercise G

1 A transistor radio is priced at £9·50. What would it cost if 10% were allowed off the marked price for paying cash?

2 By drawing a suitable tree diagram find the probability that exactly 2 tails occur when three pennies are tossed.

3 What is the image of each of the following points after reflection in *y* = 0?

(a) (1, 2);   (b) (3, ⁻2);   (c) (⁻3, 0).

4 Find the area of a sector of angle 120° cut off from a circle of radius 21 mm.

5 Is the network in Figure 2 traversable? Give a reason for your answer.

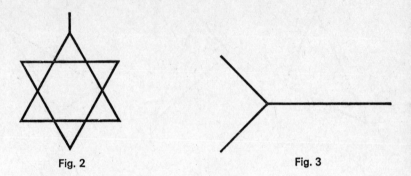

Fig. 2   Fig. 3

6 What is the least number of line segment(s) which must be added to Figure 3 to give it just two lines of symmetry? On a copy of the figure, show where the segment(s) must be drawn.

7 Solve the following equations:

(a) $x - 5 = 2$; (b) $3x + 4 = 19$; (c) $\frac{2}{5}x = 18$; (d) $12 - x = {}^{-}2$.

8 The burning lives in hours for 10 light bulbs were found to be as follows:

850, 900, 1370, 1080, 1060, 860, 1060, 1040, 1090, 1930.

Find the mean life.

Exercise H (Multi-choice)

In this exercise there may be more than one correct answer to a question. Write down the letter (or letters) corresponding to the correct answer (or answers). Show any rough working that you do.

1 The value of $7\cdot521 \div 1000$ is

(a) $0\cdot07521$; (b) $0\cdot0007521$; (c) $0\cdot007521$; (d) none of these.

2 Three of the four networks in Figure 4 are topologically equivalent. Which one is not topologically equivalent to the other three?

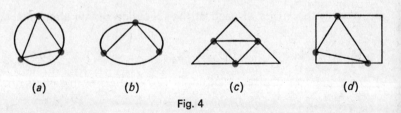

(a)   (b)   (c)   (d)

Fig. 4

3 Which of the following fractions is the largest?

(a) $\frac{2}{5}$;   (b) $\frac{1}{3}$;   (c) $\frac{2}{7}$;   (d) $\frac{3}{8}$.

4 Which of the following statements *must* be true for the triangle in Figure 5?

(a) $AB^2 + AC^2 = BC^2$;

(b) $AC^2 - AB^2 = BC^2$;

(c) $AB^2 + BC^2 = AC^2$;

(d) AB is the longest side.

Fig. 5

5 'Passengers are allowed 20 kg free of charge; any amount in excess of 20 kg is charged at 5p per kg.'

If W kg is the weight of the luggage (to the nearest kg) and C pence is the cost, the relation above is described by the formula

(a) $C = 5(W+20)$;   (b) $C = 5W - 20$;

(c) $C = 5(W-20)$;   (d) none of these.

6 When a record is being played the path traced by the stylus is

(a) a straight line;   (b) a circle;   (c) a spiral;   (d) none of these.

Exercise I

1 The square $OPQR$ is mapped onto the quadrilateral $OPXY$ by the shear S. (See Figure 6.) Y is the mid-point of RQ and $OR = 4$ cm.

(a) What kind of quadrilateral is $OPXY$?

(b) Write down the area of $OPXY$.

(c) On a copy of Figure 6, draw the image of the quadrilateral $OPXY$ under the shear S.

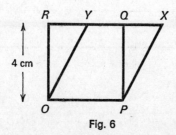

Fig. 6

2 A ship sails for 85 km on a bearing of 310°. It then changes course and sails for a further 130 km on a bearing of 215°. Draw a sketch of the ship's route. Calculate how far its final position is

(a) east or west of the starting position;

(b) north or south of the starting position.

3 The formula for finding the nth triangle number is

$$\tfrac{1}{2}n(n+1).$$

Use the formula to find

(a) the 4th triangle number;

(b) the 99th triangle number;

(c) the sum of the counting numbers from 1 to 100.

4 (a) Draw a diagram to show the effect of the matrix $\begin{pmatrix} 1 & ^-2 \\ 1 & 1 \end{pmatrix}$ on the parallelogram in Figure 7. What is the shape of the image?

(b) Draw a second diagram to show the effect of the matrix $\begin{pmatrix} \frac{1}{2} & 0 \\ 0 & \frac{1}{2} \end{pmatrix}$ on the parallelogram in Figure 7. Describe the transformation which this matrix represents.

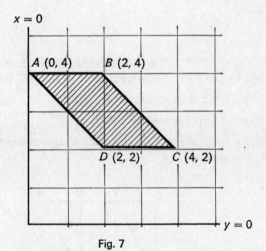

Fig. 7

5   The four transformations which map the rectangle in Figure 8(a) onto itself are as follows:

  I, the identity transformation;

  P, reflection in the line p;

  Q, reflection in the line q;

  R, rotation through 180° about O.

Copy and complete the table in Figure 8(b).

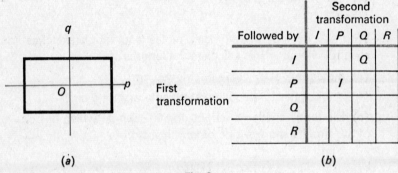

	Second transformation			
Followed by	I	P	Q	R
I			Q	
P	I			
Q				
R				

First transformation

(a)   (b)

Fig. 8

(a) Is the set {I, P, Q, R} closed under the operation 'followed by'?

(b) What is the inverse of (i) P, (ii) Q, (iii) R?

6   The pages in a book are numbered from 1 to 200. Copy and complete the following table to show the frequencies of pages whose numbers have 1, 2, and 3 digits.

Number of digits	1	2	3
Frequency			

(a) State the modal number of digits.

(b) State the median number of digits.

(c) Calculate the mean number of digits.

(d) A page is chosen at random. What is the probability that its number will contain just two digits?

(e) A page is chosen at random from those with 2-digit numbers. What is the probability that one of its digits will be zero?

Revision exercises

Exercise J

1 Triangle ABC has vertices $A(0, 1)$, $B(2, 1)$, $C(2, 4)$. Draw this triangle on centimetre squared paper choosing values of x between 0 and 5 and values of y between $^-3$ and 4.

    Describe in words the shear which maps triangle ABC onto a triangle with vertices at:

  (a) (0, 1), (2, 1), (5, 4);

  (b) (0, 1), (0, $^-2$), (2, 4);

  (c) (2, 1), (2, 4), (0, $^-3$).

2 With the help of trigonometry tables and rough sketches (and a slide rule if you wish), calculate the lengths of:

  (a) a diagonal of a square of side 4·5 cm;

  (b) the height of an equilateral triangle of side 6 cm;

  (c) the longest side of a right-angled triangle which has one angle of 35° and its shortest side of length 7 cm.

3 The cost in pounds (C) of hiring a car is given by the formula

$$C = 10 + \frac{2n}{75}$$

where n is the number of km travelled.

  (a) What is the total cost if the car is driven only 1500 km?

  (b) What is the average cost per km for a distance of 1500 km?

  (c) What is the average cost per km if the car travels 3000 km?

  (d) Does the cost per km become larger or smaller as the distance increases?

  (e) If the total cost is £30, how far has the car travelled?

4 (a) Draw a square with vertices at $A(0, 0)$, $B(1, 0)$, $C(1, 1)$ and $D(0, 1)$.

  (b) Draw a diagram to show the effect of the matrix $\begin{pmatrix} 1 & 3 \\ 0 & 1 \end{pmatrix}$ on $ABCD$. Label the image $A_1B_1C_1D_1$.

  (c) What transformation does $\begin{pmatrix} 1 & 3 \\ 0 & 1 \end{pmatrix}$ represent?

  (d) Now transform $A_1B_1C_1D_1$ by the matrix $\begin{pmatrix} 1 & ^-3 \\ 0 & 1 \end{pmatrix}$ and show the new image on your diagram. What happens?

(e) What can you say about the matrices $\begin{pmatrix} 1 & 3 \\ 0 & 1 \end{pmatrix}$ and $\begin{pmatrix} 1 & -3 \\ 0 & 1 \end{pmatrix}$?

Check that $\begin{pmatrix} 1 & -3 \\ 0 & 1 \end{pmatrix}\begin{pmatrix} 1 & 3 \\ 0 & 1 \end{pmatrix} = \begin{pmatrix} 1 & 0 \\ 0 & 1 \end{pmatrix}$.

5 (a) $n(A \cup B) = 80$, $n(A) = 39$ and $n(B) = 65$. Draw a diagram with two overlapping curves representing sets A and B. What is $n(A \cap B)$?

(b) List the members of the following sets:

$$P = \{\text{prime numbers less than 40}\},$$
$$F = \{\text{factors of 40}\},$$
$$S = \{\text{square numbers less than 40}\},$$
$$T = \{\text{triangle numbers less than 40}\}.$$

(c) Find

(i) $P \cap F$;   (ii) $F \cap S$;   (iii) $S \cap T$;   (iv) $P \cup F$.

6 The scale of a map is 1 to 500 000.

(a) What distance (in kilometres) is represented by

(i) 1 cm,   (ii) 6·5 cm on the map?

(b) What area (in square kilometres) is represented by

(i) 1 cm², (ii) 4 cm² on the map?

(c) What area on the map represents an area of 125 km²?

9. Percentages

1. REVISION

You did some work on percentages in *Book D*. What does the word 'percentage' mean?

'Cent' comes from the Latin word for a hundred. How many words can you think of which have 'cent', meaning a hundred, as one of their syllables?

If you score 57% in an exam it means that you get 57 out of a hundred or that you get $\frac{57}{100}$ of the total marks.

If the exam was marked out of 200 you would get $\frac{57}{100}$ of 200 = 114 marks.

Copy and complete the following five examples.

(*a*) Change 80% to a fraction:

$$80\% = \frac{}{100} = \frac{4}{5}.$$

(*b*) Change $\frac{21}{25}$ to a percentage:

$$\frac{21}{25} = \frac{21 \times 4}{25 \times 4} = \frac{}{100} = 84\%.$$

(*c*) Change 0·3 to a percentage:

$$0\cdot3 = \frac{3}{10} = \quad \%.$$

(*d*) Work out 30% of £6.

$$30\% \text{ of } £6 = \frac{30}{100} \text{ of } £6$$

$$= \frac{}{10} \text{ of } £6.$$

$\frac{1}{10}$ of £6 = 60p.

So $\quad\quad\quad \frac{3}{10}$ of £6 = .

Therefore, 30% of £6 is £1·80.

(*e*) In a sale the price of an article is reduced by 25%. If its original price was £8, what is its new price?

$$25\% \text{ of } £8 = \frac{25}{100} \text{ of } £8$$

$$= \tfrac{1}{4} \text{ of } £8$$

$$= £ \quad .$$

The new price is £8 – £ = £ .

Exercise A

1 Change these percentages to fractions in their simplest form (see Example (*a*)).

 (*a*) 60%;   (*b*) 24%;   (*c*) 33⅓%;   (*d*) 79%.

2 Change these fractions to percentages (see Example (*b*)).

 (*a*) $\frac{1}{2}$;   (*b*) $\frac{67}{100}$;   (*c*) $\frac{3}{4}$;   (*d*) $\frac{27}{50}$.

3 Change these decimals to percentages (see Example (*c*)).

 (*a*) 0·4;   (*b*) 0·25;   (*c*) 0·87;   (*d*) 0·1.

4 Work out, as in Example (*d*):

 (*a*) 20% of £6;   (*b*) 50% of 64 km;

 (*c*) 65% of £300;   (*d*) 37% of £2.

5 (*a*) 30% of children in a school have had measles. What percentage has not had measles?

 (*b*) If the school has 650 pupils, how many children have not had measles?

6 A boy got 20 out of 50 for History, 60 out of 80 for Maths, 45 out of 60 for Geography and 21 out of 25 for English. Write these marks as percentages and so find out which is his best mark.

7 In a sale the price of a pair of shoes is reduced by 20%. If the original price was £4·50, what is the reduction? What is the sale price? (See Example (*e*).)

8 In a sale all prices are reduced by 15%. Find the new prices of articles which originally cost:

(*a*) £5;   (*b*) 80p;   (*c*) £6·40.

9 Mr B. buys a car for £1250 and pays a deposit of 20%. How much does he still have to pay?

10 Mr P. puts money into a bank savings account which pays 6% interest per year.

(*a*) If he puts in £250, how much interest does he get in the first year?

(*b*) How much money does he have in his account at the end of the first year?

2. FINDING PERCENTAGES OF AMOUNTS OF MONEY

There is an easy way of working out percentages of amounts of money. As there are 100p in £1, 1% of £1 = 1p.

What is 1% of £2?

What is 1% of £15?

You could find 3% of £6 by saying:

$$1\% \text{ of } £6 = 6p,$$

so $$3\% \text{ of } £6 = 3 \times 6p = 18p.$$

Example 1

To find $3\frac{1}{2}\%$ of £24:

$$1\% \text{ of } £24 = 24p,$$

so $3\frac{1}{2}\%$ of £24 $= 3\frac{1}{2} \times 24p$

$$= 84p.$$

Work out:

(*a*) 6% of £31;   (*b*) $3\frac{1}{2}\%$ of £21;   (*c*) $4\frac{1}{2}\%$ of £16.

This method will still work even if we do not start with a whole number of pounds.

Example 2

To find $4\frac{1}{2}$% of £18·40:

$$1\% \text{ of } £18·40 = 18·40\text{p}$$

$$4\frac{1}{2}\% \text{ of } £18·40 = 4\frac{1}{2} \times 18·40\text{p}$$

$$= 82·80\text{p}$$

$$= 83\text{p to the nearest penny.}$$

3. PRACTICAL USES OF PERCENTAGES

3.1 National Savings Bank accounts

If you have money in a National Savings Bank account you will get $3\frac{1}{2}$% interest each year. ($3\frac{1}{2}$% is called the interest rate.)

Using the method of Section 2, work out how much interest you would receive in one year if you had in your account:

(a) £6;   (b) £15;   (c) £220.

Suppose you put £20 into your account at the beginning of a year. In the first year you would get $3\frac{1}{2}$% of £20 interest.

Check that this is 70p interest.

So, at the beginning of the second year, you would have £20·70 in your account. In the second year the interest would be, not 70p again, but $3\frac{1}{2}$% of £20·70.

$$1\% \text{ of } £20·70 = 20·70\text{p}.$$

So $3\frac{1}{2}\% \text{ of } £20·70 = 3\frac{1}{2} \times 20·70\text{p}$

$$= ?\text{ p}$$

$$= ?\text{ p to the nearest penny.}$$

How much money, to the nearest penny, would be in your account at the end of the second year?

This method of paying interest is called *Compound Interest*. You get more interest each year – provided you leave all the money in. If the National Savings Bank only paid you the same interest – 70p – each year it would be paying *Simple Interest*.

Copy and complete the two diagrams in Figure 1 to show how much money you would have, by Compound Interest and by Simple Interest, after three years. Do all the calculations to the nearest penny.

121

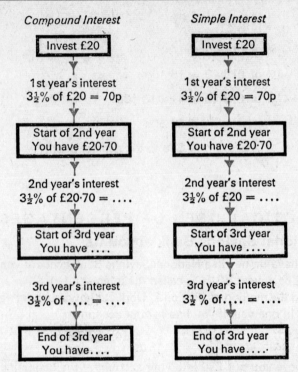

Fig. 1

3.2 Investing at a higher interest rate

The National Savings Bank pays a low rate of interest. It is possible to invest money at a higher rate, but there are sometimes snags about these methods. It might be necessary to invest a fairly large amount of money or it might not be easy to draw your money out when you needed it. You might like to try to find out about some of these ways of investing money.

In Section 3.1 you might have thought that it was not worth the trouble of working out Compound Interest, since there was so little difference between Compound and Simple Interest. However, if you get a higher rate of interest and invest a larger amount of money, the difference will be quite noticeable.

Suppose you invested £500 and the interest rate was 8%. Work out how much money you would have at the end of three years by Compound and by Simple Interest. You might find it helpful to do the working in a diagram like Figure 1.

3.3 No Claims Bonuses

Most Car Insurance Companies offer a No-Claims Bonus Scheme. This means that if you have no accidents and so do not need to claim any money, you pay less for your insurance in the following year. One possible scheme is as follows:

After 1 year with no claim   reduction is 25%.
After 2 consecutive years with no claim   reduction is $33\frac{1}{3}$%.
After 3 consecutive years with no claim   reduction is 40%.
After 4 consecutive years with no claim   reduction is 50%.

All the reductions are worked out as a percentage of the original amount you pay. This is called the *premium*.

The following working shows the amount paid at the beginning of each year if the premium was £24 and assuming you had no accidents.

1st year   You pay the premium, £24.

2nd year

Bonus $= \frac{25}{100}$ of £24 $= \frac{1}{4}$ of £24 $=$ £6.   You pay £24 − £6 $=$ £18.

3rd year

Bonus $= \dfrac{33\frac{1}{3}}{100}$ of £24 $= \frac{1}{3}$ of £24 $=$ £8.   You pay £24 − £8 $=$ £16.

4th year

Bonus $= \frac{40}{100}$ of £24 $= \frac{2}{5}$ of £24 $=$ £9·60.
                                 You pay £24 − £9·60 $=$ £14·40.

5th year

Bonus $= \frac{50}{100}$ of £24 $= \frac{1}{2}$ of £24 $=$ £12.   You pay £24 − £12 $=$ £12.

After this, you would pay £12 each year, provided you did not have an accident.

Work out how much you would pay in each of the first 5 years if the same Bonus Scheme was used but your premium was £30.

3.4 Building Societies

If you wanted to buy a house you would probably borrow money from a Building Society. The Society would charge you about 8 or 9% interest on the money you borrowed.

Suppose you borrowed £3000 at an interest rate of 9%, and were to pay back £7·50 a week to the Society.

Each year you would pay £7·50 × 52 $=$ £390.

You might think that at the end of the first year you would owe the Society £3000 − £390 $=$ £2610. *But* this is not so.

The Society will take 9% of the £3000 you owe at the beginning of the year as interest:

$$9\% \text{ of } £3000 = £270.$$

This has to be deducted from the £390 before you begin to pay off the loan. £390 − £270 = £120, so in the first year £120 will be paid off the loan.

At the end of the first year you would owe the Society

$$£3000 - £120 = £2880.$$

In the second year things are *slightly* better, as the Society will take 9% of the money you owe at the beginning of the year as interest, that is,

$$\tfrac{9}{100} \text{ of } £2880 = £259·20.$$

You would again pay £390, so this year £390 − £259·20 = £130·80 would be paid off the loan.

You would then owe £2880 − £130·80 = £2749·20.

This table shows the working for the first two years.

		Money you owe the Society £3000
1st Year	You pay £390 Interest due, $\tfrac{9}{100}$ of £3000 = £270 Amount taken off loan = £120	
		£2880
2nd Year	You pay £390 Interest due, $\tfrac{9}{100}$ of £2880 = £259·20 Amount taken off loan = £130·80	
		£2749·20

Continue this working to show the amounts owed after each of the next few years. Notice that each year the interest is less, so you pay off more of the loan.

To keep the working simple, assume that each year you would pay off any odd fractions of a pound. For example, after the second year you would pay an extra 20p and so owe exactly £2749.

You might like to use a calculating machine to help with the working. If you do this, try to continue the working to see how long it would take to pay off the loan. How much money would you pay to the Society altogether?

3.5 Other uses of percentages

There are many other occasions on which you are likely to meet percentages. Look out for examples of percentages in advertisements, shops and newspapers, and listen for references to them on T.V. or radio. Whenever you find an example, try to work out what it really means.

Here are some possibilities:

(*a*) 'They have been given a pay rise of $6\frac{1}{2}$%'. How much extra would a man get who was earning £25 a week?

(*b*) '6% of his salary is paid to a Superannuation Fund'. (What is a Superannuation Fund?)

How much a year would a man pay if his salary was £1500? How much would he pay each week (to the nearest penny)?

(*c*) Sometimes percentages are written differently. For example, an interest rate might be given as £5·30 per cent. This means that if you invest £100 you get £5·30 interest at the end of the year. How much would you get in a year if you invested £350?

4. FINDING PERCENTAGES

Four Youth Clubs in neighbouring villages decided to try to increase their membership. There was to be a prize for the club which got the best improvement in numbers.

Here are the results:

	Original membership	Final membership	Increase
Club *A*	40	50	10
Club *B*	20	28	8
Club *C*	60	80	20
Club *D*	10	15	5

Who should win the prize?

Club *C* had the most new members, but they probably came from the largest village. In any case they had more people to look for new members. It would be fairer to compare the number of new members with the original size of the club. One way is to give the increase as a fraction of the original size.

Fractional increase

Club *A*	$\frac{10}{40} = \frac{1}{4}$
Club *B*	$\frac{8}{20} = ?$
Club *C*	$\frac{20}{60} = ?$
Club *D*	$\frac{5}{10} = ?$

Work out the fractions for Clubs *B*, *C* and *D*.

It is still not very easy to see who did best and it would be better to change the fractions to percentages.

	Fractional increase	Percentage increase
Club *A*	$\frac{1}{4}$	25%
Club *B*	$\frac{2}{5}$	?
Club *C*	$\frac{1}{3}$	?
Club *D*	$\frac{1}{2}$	?

Work out the percentages for Clubs *B*, *C* and *D*.

It is now obvious that, relative to its size, Club *D* did best and so should win the prize.

Exercise B

1   The population of a new town was 10000 in 1960 and 16000 in 1970. What was the increase in population? What was this as a fraction of the original size? What was the percentage increase in the ten years?

2   28 out of a class of 35 wanted to take part in a project.
(*a*) What percentage of the class was this?
(*b*) In another class, 24 out of 32 wanted to take part. What percentage was this? Which class was the keener?

3   A shopkeeper bought an article for £6 and sold it for £8.
(*a*) What profit did he make?
(*b*) Write this as a fraction of the price the shop paid.
(*c*) Change this fraction to a percentage. This is called the percentage profit.

4   Find the percentage profits on these articles:
(*a*) bought for £6 and sold for £9;
(*b*) bought for £32 and sold for £40;
(*c*) bought for 30p and sold for 36p.

5   A book is 200 mm long to the nearest mm. A girl measures it rather carelessly and gets 190 mm.
(*a*) What is her error?
(*b*) Write this as a percentage of the correct value. This is called the percentage error.

6   Some young boys were practising measuring by trying to find the lengths of ropes:

John had 520 cm instead of 500 cm.

Peter had 290 cm instead of 300 cm.

Robert had 53 cm instead of 50 cm.

Find the percentage error for each boy. Who do you think measured most accurately?

10. Waves

1. THE SINE CURVE

1.1 The rotating wheel

You will need a wheel, such as a bicycle wheel, mounted vertically on its axle with a plumb line attached to a point P on the rim. See Figure 1.

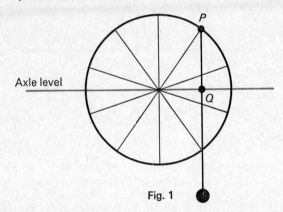

Axle level

Fig. 1

Suppose the wheel starts with P at the same level as the axle. As the wheel rotates, the height of P above this level can be found by measuring the length PQ on the plumb line.

To begin with, the height of P is zero.

When does the height of P have its greatest value?

When is the height of P zero again?

When the wheel has turned through $45°$, is the height of P half of its greatest height?

Draw a rough graph showing how the height of P varies as the angle changes. (The axes are shown in Figure 2.)

127

What happens to the height of *P* as the angle goes beyond 180°?

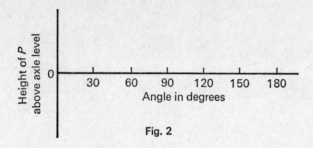

Fig. 2

1.2 Calculating the height

It is possible to *calculate* the height of the point *P*.

Suppose the wheel had turned through 40° as in Figure 3. Then, with the axes as shown and taking the radius of the wheel as 1 unit, the *y*-coordinate of the point *P* would be sin 40°.

Look up 40° in your sine tables.

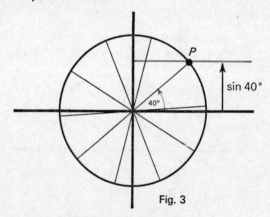

Fig. 3

Use your tables to complete the following table:

Angle turned through	Height of *P*
0°	0·000
10°	
20°	
30°	
40°	0·643
50°	
60°	
70°	
80°	
90°	1·000

Use the information you have just obtained to draw a graph with axes as shown in Figure 4. Suggested scales are 1 cm for 20° across the page and 1 cm for 0·2 up the page. Ignore the angles from 90° to 360° : we shall deal with these in the next section.

Compare your rough graph from Section 1.1 with this one.

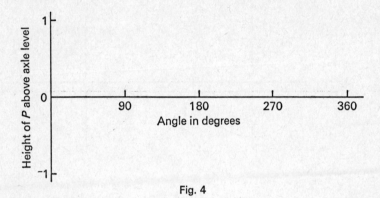

Fig. 4

1.3   Angles greater than 90°

Is it possible to look up sin 100° in your book of tables ? Suggest a meaning for sin 100°.

Here is a method for finding sin 100° :

When the wheel has rotated through 100°, the height of *P* will be exactly the same as it was at 80°, that is, the height will be sin 80°. (See Figure 5.) This means that sin 100° has the same value as sin 80°.

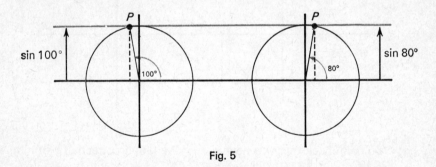

Fig. 5

As the wheel turns from 90° to 180° the height of *P* decreases. When the angle is 110° the height will be the same as it was at 70°, that is, sin 70°.

When the angle is 120°, what will the height be ?

Use this method to continue your graph up to 180°. You should get a symmetrical curve.

129

When the angle is greater than 180°, the height of P becomes negative. See Figure 6.

At angle 190°, for example, the height is the same as at 10°, except that it is negative. From tables, sin 10° is 0·174. Hence sin 190° = ⁻0·174.

Use this method to continue your graph as far as 270°.

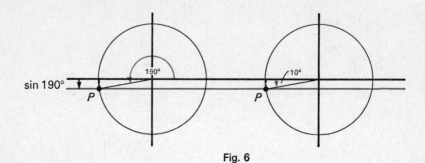

Fig. 6

When the angle increases beyond 270°, the height of P is still negative. At 300°, for example, the height is the same as at 60°, except that it is negative. (See Figure 7.) From tables, sin 60° is 0·866. Hence

$$\sin 300° = {}^-0·866.$$

Continue your graph as far as 360°.

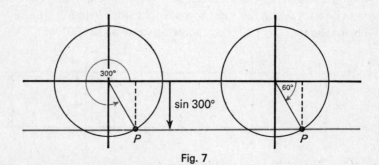

Fig. 7

You can check that you have drawn the graph correctly by turning to page 18 of the *S.M.P. Elementary Tables*.

The graph you have drawn is a graph of the mapping

$$x \rightarrow \sin x°.$$

It is called a sine curve.

How would you expect it to continue beyond 360°?

Describe the symmetries of the curve.

Exercise A

1 Read off from your graph the sines of the following angles:

   (a) 45°;   (b) 135°;   (c) 225°;   (d) 315°.

2 (a) Read off from your graph angles whose sines are 0·6.

   (b) Read off angles whose sines are ⁻0·6.

3 Figure 5 showed that the sine of 100° has the same value as the sine of 80°. Write down angles between 0° and 90° which would help you to find the sines of the following angles:

   (a) 125°;   (b) 173°;   (c) 205°;   (d) 265°;   (e) 327°.

4 Use your answers to Question 3, and a book of tables to find

   (a) sin 125°;   (b) sin 173°;   (c) sin 205°;   (d) sin 265°;

   (e) sin 327°.

5 Find all the angles between 0° and 360° whose sines are

   (a) 0·500;   (b) ⁻0·500;   (c) 0·477;   (d) ⁻0·632.

6 In the previous work we called the radius of the wheel 1 unit. Take the radius as 33 cm and find the height of the point P above its starting position (level with the axle) when the wheel has turned through (a) 50°; (b) 110°. (See Figure 8.)

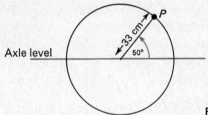

Fig. 8

7 A graph of $x \rightarrow \cos x°$ can be drawn in the following way:

   When the wheel has turned through 40°, the horizontal distance of P from the centre (that is, the x-coordinate of P) is cos 40°, which is 0·766. (See Figure 9.)

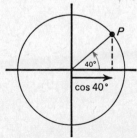

Fig. 9

What is the *x*-coordinate of *P* when the wheel has turned through 50°?

On your diagram of the sine curve draw, in a different colour, a graph showing how this horizontal distance of *P* from the axle varies for angles between 0° and 90°.

8 When the wheel has rotated through 100°, the *x*-coordinate of the point *P* is the same as when it had rotated through 80° except that it is negative. Use this method to continue the graph up to 360°.

9 Compare the graphs of $x \to \sin x°$ and $x \to \cos x°$.
How could one be mapped onto the other?

10 Write down the angles between 0° and 90° which would help you to find the cosines of the following angles:

(*a*) 115°;   (*b*) 165°;   (*c*) 238°;   (*d*) 324°.

11 Use your answers to Question 10, and a book of tables to find:

(*a*) cos 115°;   (*b*) cos 165°;   (*c*) cos 238°;   (*d*) cos 324°.

12 Find all the angles between 0° and 360° whose cosines are:

(*a*) 0·500;   (*b*) ⁻0·500;   (*c*) 0·216;   (*d*) ⁻0·798.

2. WAVES

The title of this chapter probably made you think of the seaside and the waves of the sea. The height of a point on a wheel varies in a wave-like manner, and the same type of pattern occurs in many other situations. All of these are connected with the sine curve. Here are some scientific examples of sine waves:

Investigation 1

(*a*) You will need a piece of rope about 5 metres long. Attach one end to a fixed object such as a door-knob. Stretch the rope out and move the other end in a circular motion. See Figure 10.

Waves will be set up. Notice how they travel along the rope.

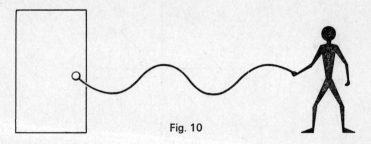

Fig. 10

(*b*) Carry out some experiments with a 'slinky'.

Investigation 2

Some diaries give the times of sunset and sunrise, usually for every Saturday in the year.

Draw a graph showing the times of sunrise with axes as shown in Figure 11. (Suggested scales : 2 mm for each week across the page, 1 cm for each hour up the page.)

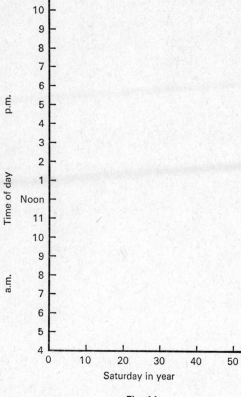

Fig. 11

On the same diagram draw another graph for the times of sunset.

Try to find out why the times of sunset and sunrise should vary in a wave-like manner.

Find the lengths of the longest and shortest days.

Investigation 3

(*a*) The table shows the approximate height of the tide at Swansea for part of a day in 1969.

Time of day	Height of tide in metres
7.00	9·0
8.00	8·6
9.00	6·8
10.00	4·8
11.00	2·4
12.00	0·7
13.00	0·1
14.00	0·9
15.00	2·5
16.00	4·7
17.00	7·0
18.00	8·9
19.00	9·4
20.00	8·9
21.00	7·4
22.00	4·9
23.00	2·5
0.00	0·8
1.00	0·0

Draw a graph of these heights with axes as in Figure 12. (Suggested scales: 1 cm for each hour across the page, 1 cm for each metre up the page.)

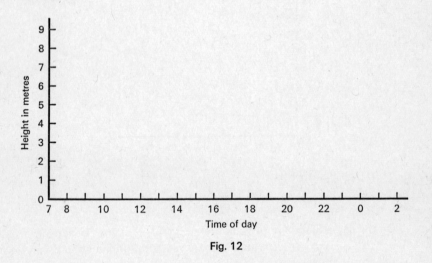

Fig. 12

Try to explain why this wave-like variation should take place.

At what time of day was it (i) high tide, (ii) low tide?

During what times would it have been possible for a ship drawing 4 m of water to enter the harbour?

What was the average level of the tide?

When was the tide rising?

When was the tide falling most rapidly?

(*b*) The next table shows the greatest height of the tide at Swansea for a period of 30 days in 1969.

Day	Height of tide in metres	Day	Height of tide in metres
1	8·7	16	8·4
2	8·5	17	8·3
3	8·1	18	8·2
4	7·7	19	7·9
5	7·2	20	7·4
6	6·7	21	6·9
7	6·5	22	6·7
8	6·6	23	6·9
9	6·9	24	7·5
10	7·3	25	8·1
11	7·7	26	8·7
12	7·9	27	9·0
13	8·2	28	9·1
14	8·3	29	9·0
15	8·4	30	8·8

Draw a graph to show this information. (Suggested scales: 0·5 cm for every day across the page, 4 cm for 1 m up the page.)

Investigation 4

(*a*) Find out about the motion of a pendulum.

(*b*) Find out about the up-and-down motion of a weight suspended on a spring.

(*c*) All sounds are caused by vibrations. Find out about the vibrations of musical instruments.

(*d*) Look at a long playing record through a magnifying glass, or find a photograph showing a magnification of a record.

(*d*) What do the letters V.H.F. stand for?

(*f*) The electricity in your house is probably 240 volts A.C. What does A.C. stand for?

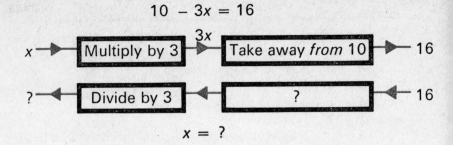

$$10 - 3x = 16$$

11. Solution of equations

You have already learned how to solve equations like $10 - 3x = 16$, $2x + 3 = 6$, $3(x - 4) = 9$ and $3(6 - x) = 8$. Make sure you can still do these – the flow diagram above will help you with the first.

In this chapter you will learn how to solve equations like

$$\frac{6}{x} = {}^-2, \quad \frac{7}{2x} = 1 \quad \text{and} \quad 2\left(\frac{6}{x} + 3\right) = 10.$$

Can you see what makes these equations different from the ones you have met before?

1. NEGATIVE NUMBERS

Make sure you get the questions in Exercise A correct before going on.

Exercise A

1 $^-4 + 7$.

2 $^-8 + 2$.

3 $^-6 - 3$.

4 Take 4 away from $^-6$.

5 Take $^-2$ away from 5.

6 Take $^-6$ away from $^-3$.

7 $6 \times {}^-3$.

8 $^-3 \times {}^-5$.

9 $6 \div {}^-3$.

10 $^-12 \div {}^-3$.

11 $^-8 \div 4$.

12 Divide 3 into 15.

13 Divide 3 into $^-15$.

14 Divide $^-4$ into 12.

15 Divide $^-4$ into $^-12$.

16 Divide $^-8$ into 4.

17 $2 \div \frac{1}{2}$.

18 $3 \div {}^-\frac{1}{4}$.

19 Divide $\frac{1}{3}$ into 2.

20 Divide $^-\frac{1}{2}$ into 4.

2. MAPPINGS AND THEIR INVERSES

In the *Book F* chapter on equations we found that it helped to look at mappings like $x \to 6-x$, which were self-inverse.

For the new equations in this chapter, which you should have noticed all involve dividing by x, we are going to use mappings again.

Figure 1 (*a*) shows the mapping diagram for

$$x \to \frac{6}{x}.$$

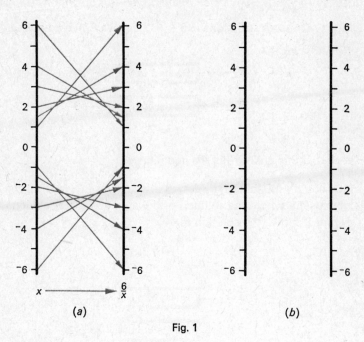

$x \xrightarrow{\hspace{2cm}} \frac{6}{x}$

(*a*)   (*b*)

Fig. 1

Why is there no arrow going from 0? Copy Figures 1 (*a*) and 1 (*b*) and complete (*b*) to show the inverse mapping for

$$x \to \frac{6}{x}.$$

Draw diagrams for the mapping $x \to \dfrac{12}{x}$ and its inverse.

You should see that both $x \to \dfrac{6}{x}$ and $x \to \dfrac{12}{x}$ are self-inverse mappings.

Do you think $x \to \dfrac{8}{x}$ is a self-inverse mapping?

3. EQUATIONS SUCH AS $\frac{6}{x} = 3$

We can now set about solving the equation $\frac{6}{x} = 3$.

First we must write out the flow diagrams.
We start with x and divide it *into* 6:

$$x \longrightarrow \boxed{\text{Divide } \textit{into } 6} \longrightarrow 3$$

Just as $x \rightarrow \frac{6}{x}$ is a *self-inverse mapping*, so the operation 'Divide *into* 6' which we meet in equations like $\frac{6}{x} = 3$, is a *self inverse operation*.

So we have:

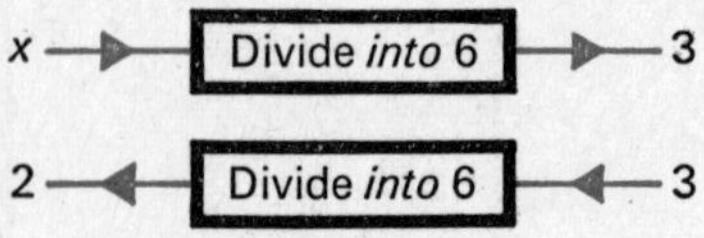

$$x \longrightarrow \boxed{\text{Divide } \textit{into } 6} \longrightarrow 3$$

$$2 \longleftarrow \boxed{\text{Divide } \textit{into } 6} \longleftarrow 3$$

$$x = 2.$$

Check that this answer fits the equation.

You could probably have spotted this answer anyway, but the method is very useful where the solution of the equation is not obvious.
Figure 2 shows the solution for

$$\frac{6}{x} = {}^-3.$$

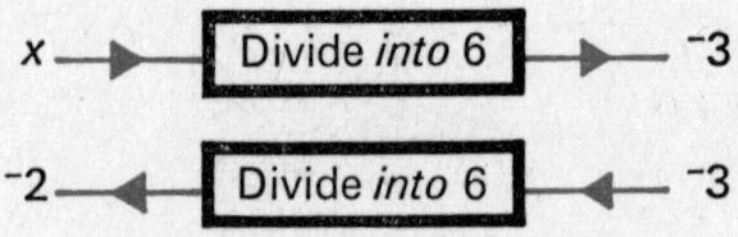

$$x \longrightarrow \boxed{\text{Divide } \textit{into } 6} \longrightarrow {}^-3$$

$${}^-2 \longleftarrow \boxed{\text{Divide } \textit{into } 6} \longleftarrow {}^-3$$

$$x = {}^-2.$$

Fig. 2

Copy and complete Figure 3 for $\frac{{}^-8}{x} = 4$ and check that your answer fits the equation.

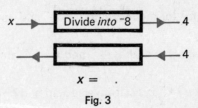

$$x \longrightarrow \boxed{\text{Divide } \textit{into } {}^-8} \longrightarrow 4$$

$$\longleftarrow \boxed{\phantom{\text{Divide } \textit{into } {}^-8}} \longleftarrow 4$$

$$x = \quad .$$

Fig. 3

Exercise B

Solve each of these equations by drawing flow diagrams.

1   $\dfrac{12}{x} = 2.$ 2 $\dfrac{^-12}{x} = 2.$ 3 $\dfrac{6}{x} = 4.$

4   $\dfrac{4}{x} = {}^-2.$ 5 $\dfrac{9}{x} = 4.$ 6 $\dfrac{^-20}{x} = {}^-4.$

7   $\dfrac{^-7}{x} = 3.$ 8 $\dfrac{5}{x} = {}^-3.$ 9 $\dfrac{2}{x} = \tfrac{1}{2}.$

10   $\dfrac{4}{x} = \tfrac{1}{3}.$

4. EQUATIONS SUCH AS $\dfrac{6}{x} + 1 = 3$ AND $\dfrac{14}{3x} = 2$

Figure 4 shows the flow diagram to solve

$$\frac{6}{x} + 1 = 3.$$

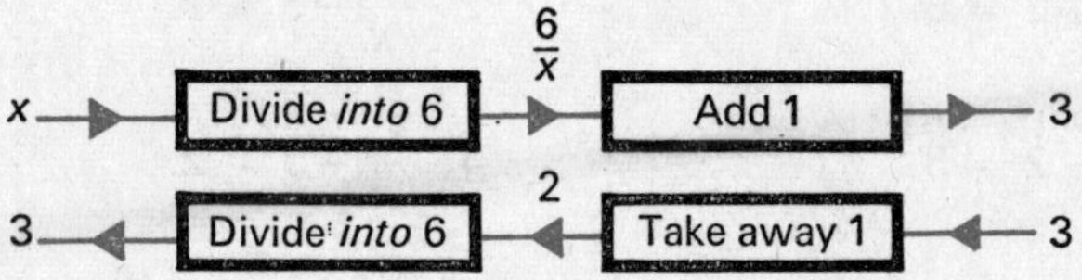

x ⟶ | Divide *into* 6 | ⟶ $\frac{6}{x}$ | Add 1 | ⟶ 3

3 ⟵ | Divide *into* 6 | ⟵ 2 | Take away 1 | ⟵ 3

$x = 3.$

Fig. 4

('Take away 1' is the inverse operation for 'Add 1' and 'Divide *into* 6' is the inverse operation for 'Divide *into* 6'.)

Does the answer fit the equation?

Copy and complete Figure 5 to solve

$$\frac{8}{x} - 3 = {}^-1.$$

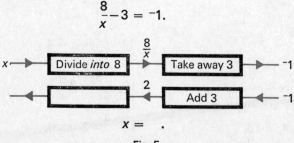

$x =$.

Fig. 5

Check that your answer fits the equation.

Copy and complete Figure 6 to solve

$$\frac{14}{3x} = 2.$$

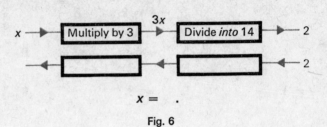

$$x = \quad .$$

Fig. 6

Check that your answer fits the equation.

Exercise C

Solve the equations in this exercise.

1   $\dfrac{12}{x} + 2 = 6.$ 2 $\dfrac{15}{x} - 3 = 2.$

3   $\dfrac{12}{x} - 2 = 3.$ 4 $\dfrac{12}{x} - 3 = 2.$

5   $\dfrac{20}{x} + 6 = 2.$ 6 $\dfrac{12}{x} + 8 = 6.$

7   $\dfrac{20}{x} - 6 = {}^{-}10.$ 8 $\dfrac{16}{x} + 2 = {}^{-}6.$

9   $\dfrac{9}{2x} = 3.$ 10 $\dfrac{8}{3x} = 2.$

11   $\dfrac{7}{2x} = 2.$ 12 $\dfrac{8}{3x} = {}^{-}2.$

13   $\dfrac{{}^{-}10}{3x} = 2.$ 14 $\dfrac{{}^{-}8}{x} + 2 = 4.$

15   $\dfrac{{}^{-}12}{x} + 4 = 2.$ 16 $\dfrac{15}{4x} = 3.$

17   $\dfrac{6}{x} + 4 = 16.$ 18 $\dfrac{4}{x} + 2 = {}^{-}6.$

19   $\dfrac{{}^{-}21}{2x} = {}^{-}7.$ 20 $\dfrac{{}^{-}10}{x} - 3 = {}^{-}5.$

5. EQUATIONS SUCH AS $12 - \dfrac{6}{x} = 9$

Can you draw the flow diagrams to solve the equation

$$12 - \frac{6}{x} = 9\,?$$

Try to do this before looking below at the answer.

You should have written:

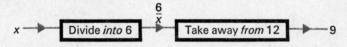

Both of these operations are self-inverse, so reversing the diagram, we get:

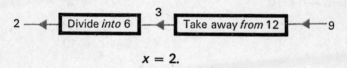

$$x = 2.$$

Check that this answer is correct.

Copy and complete the solution in Figure 7 for

$$2 - \frac{24}{x} = {}^{-}4.$$

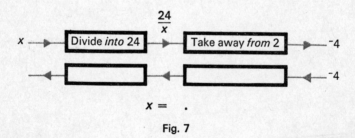

$$x = \quad .$$

Fig. 7

Exercise D

Solve the equations in this exercise. You will find that in Questions 1–12 both operations are self-inverse. In Questions 13–24 some equations will involve two self-inverse operations but others will only involve one self-inverse operation.

1   $12 - \dfrac{10}{x} = 7.$ 2 $6 - \dfrac{15}{x} = 3.$

3   $12 - \dfrac{6}{x} = 8.$ 4 $21 - \dfrac{18}{x} = 16\frac{1}{2}.$

5   $22 - \dfrac{14}{x} = 15.$ 6 $3 - \dfrac{15}{x} = {}^-2.$

7   $3 - \dfrac{20}{x} = {}^-7.$ 8 $3 - \dfrac{4}{x} = {}^-5.$

9   $6 - \dfrac{8}{x} = 10.$ 10 $5 - \dfrac{26}{x} = 7.$

11   $2 - \dfrac{6}{x} = 4.$ 12 $5 - \dfrac{20}{x} = 13.$

13   $\dfrac{20}{x} + 6 = 11.$ 14 $\dfrac{2}{x} + 3 = 7.$

15   $\dfrac{8}{x} + 3 = {}^-1.$ 16 $\dfrac{6}{x} - 5 = {}^-7.$

17   $10 - \dfrac{16}{x} = 12.$ 18 $11 - \dfrac{3}{x} = 9.$

19   $\dfrac{24}{x} - 7 = {}^-3.$ 20 $7 - \dfrac{24}{x} = 11.$

21   $6 - \dfrac{2}{x} = 0.$ 22 $7 + \dfrac{35}{x} = 12.$ (Remember that this can be written

$$\dfrac{35}{x} + 7 = 12.)$$

23   $\dfrac{11}{2x} = 2.$ 24 $\dfrac{7}{2x} + 1 = 8.$ (This will need three boxes in each flow diagram.)

6. ALL KINDS OF EQUATIONS

Exercise E contains examples of many different kinds of equations. You will have to be very careful to get the first flow diagram correct and then to think carefully whether or not the operations you have put in the boxes are self-inverse.

Copy and complete the following four examples. Make sure you have completed them correctly before going on to Exercise E.

Example 1

$$3(4-x) = {}^-9.$$

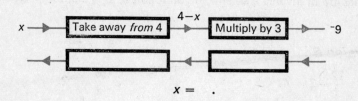

$$x = \quad .$$

(Remember, when there is a bracket, you must first do the operation which is inside it.)

Example 2

$$\tfrac{1}{3}x - 2 = 4.$$

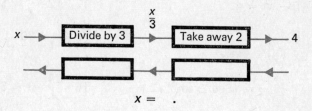

$$x = \quad .$$

Example 3

$$3\left(\frac{12}{x} + 2\right) = 15.$$

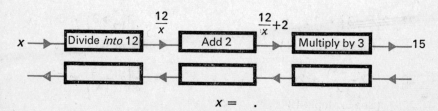

$$x = \quad .$$

143

Example 4

$$\frac{1}{2}\left(12-\frac{4}{x}\right) = 2.$$

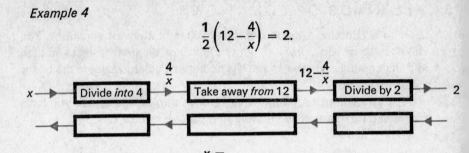

$$x = \quad .$$

You might like to answer some of the questions in Exercise E by the method of inverse elements, if you followed this method in *Book F*.

Exercise E

1 $\dfrac{12}{x} - 2 = 4.$

2 $\dfrac{8}{x} = {}^-2.$

3 $6 - 2x = 3.$

4 $2(x+3) = 8.$

5 $2x + 6 = 3.$

6 $3x + 4 = {}^-8.$

7 $8 - x = {}^-2.$

8 $3x + 2 = 9.$

9 $2(6 - x) = 8.$ (See Example 1.)

10 $8 - 2x = 10.$

11 $\frac{1}{3}(6 - x) = 4.$

12 $12 - \dfrac{8}{x} = 11.$

13 $\dfrac{16}{3x} = 4.$

14 $11 - \dfrac{30}{x} = 8.$

15 $\frac{1}{2}x - 3 = 4.$ (See Example 2.)

16 $\dfrac{24}{x} - 3 = 5.$

17 $2(8 - x) = 20.$

18 $\frac{1}{4}x - 5 = {}^-8.$

19 $3\left(\dfrac{x}{2} + 3\right) = 6.$

20 $12 - \dfrac{8}{x} = 13.$

21 $2\left(\dfrac{6}{x} + 3\right) = 10.$
(See Example 3.)

22 ${}^-3\left(\dfrac{x}{2} + 3\right) = 6.$

23 $2\left(12 - \dfrac{14}{x}\right) = 20.$
(See Example 4.)

24 $\dfrac{1}{2}\left(7 - \dfrac{18}{x}\right) = 5.$

PLAYER NO 3	1	2	3	4	5	6	7	8	9	10	TOTAL
	8 ◣	7 2	◣ 6 2	9 ◣	◢◣	◢◣	7 -	5 ◣			
	17	26	44	52	72	89	116	123			

12. Statistics

1. RUNNING TOTALS

Find the sum of 5, 9, 12, 4.

Follow through the flow diagram in Figure 1. You will probably find that your method of adding follows this pattern.

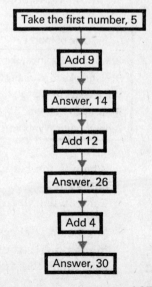

Fig. 1

A running total of these numbers can be shown in a table:

Number	Running total
5	5
9	14
12	26
4	30

Suppose that the numbers in this table represent the times taken for a journey to school. For example:

Time to walk to the station	5 minutes
Time waiting at the station for the train to arrive	9 minutes
Time spent on the train	12 minutes
Time to walk from the station to school	4 minutes

How long does it take to get to school?
How long is it from leaving home until the time that the train arrives?
How long is it from leaving home until beginning the walk from the station to school?

Exercise A

1 Copy the table below (which refers to a car journey) and complete the running total column.

Stage of journey	Distance in km	Running total	
Windsor to Basingstoke	61	Windsor to Basingstoke	61
Basingstoke to Winchester	27	Windsor to Winchester	
Winchester to Romsey	16	Windsor to Romsey	
Romsey to Ringwood	26	Windsor to Ringwood	
Ringwood to Wimborne	20	Windsor to Wimborne	

Where is the car when it is half-way between Windsor and Wimborne?
Can you describe this position in more than one way?

2 In a factory, a check was made for eight weeks on the number of cars 'turned out' each week. The manager was aiming at making 2000 cars during this time. The results were as follows:

Week	Number of cars made that week	Running total
1	197	
2	184	
3	230	
4	210	
5	280	
6	300	
7	242	
8	237	

Copy and complete the table.

(*a*) Would the manager have been pleased with the number of cars 'turned out' by the end of the fourth week?

(*b*) How many cars had been completed in

    (i) 3 weeks,   (ii) 7 weeks?

3 A boy is given his pocket money late on Friday evening. Copy and complete this table.

Day of the week	Pocket money left before going out in the morning (in pence)	Amount spent each day	Running total
Saturday	50		
Sunday	25		
Monday	22		
Tuesday	17		
Wednesday	7		
Thursday	2		
Friday	1		

2. RUNNING TOTAL GRAPHS

The table below shows the number of articles handed in to lost property during a week at school.

Day	Number of articles	Running total
Monday	6	6
Tuesday	2	8
Wednesday	3	11
Thursday	5	16
Friday	1	17

We can represent this information in a bar chart.

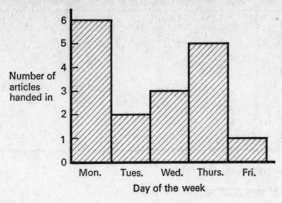

Fig 2

We can also draw a diagram to represent the running totals by piling the bars of the bar chart in Figure 2 on top of one another (see Figure 3). Check that the heights of the bars in Figure 3 agree with the entries in the table.

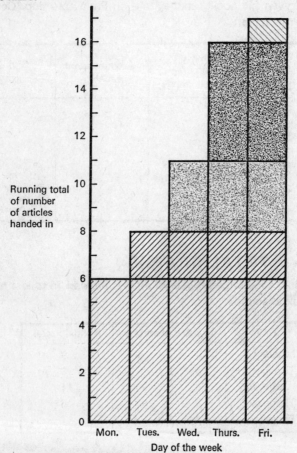

Fig. 3

Exercise B

In Questions 1–3, first copy and complete the table and then draw a running total graph like the one shown in Figure 3.

1

Week	Money saved each week in pence	Running total
1	8	
2	3	
3	8	
4	5	
5	6	
6	5	

Can you say how long it took to save 20p?

2

Throws of a dart	Score for each throw	Running total
1st	5	
2nd	16	
3rd	7	
4th	60	
5th	1	
6th	20	
7th	40	
8th	18	
9th	9	
10th	2	

In which throw did the total first exceed 100?

3

Balls bowled in cricket	Score on each stroke	Running total
1st	4	
2nd	0	
3rd	2	
4th	6	
5th	6	
6th	4	

On which ball did the batsman reach double figures for the over?

4 Do you notice anything about the general shape of each of the running total graphs you have drawn? If not, study them again carefully. Why is each bar longer than (or the same length as) the one before it?

5 This question is revision to help you with the next section.
Find the median of each of the following groups of numbers. (Remember that you must first arrange them in order and then find the middle number. If there are *two* middle numbers you must take the mean of these two numbers.)

(a) 1, 2, 4, 7, 10, 12, 13;   (b) 2, 8, 7, 9, 4;

(c) 10, 8, 11, 6, 4, 8;   (d) 7, 12, 3, 15, 2, 9;

(e) 8, 3, 5, 10, 12, 4, 7, 6, 8, 6.

3. CUMULATIVE FREQUENCY TABLES

The bar chart in Figure 4 shows the results of an examination.

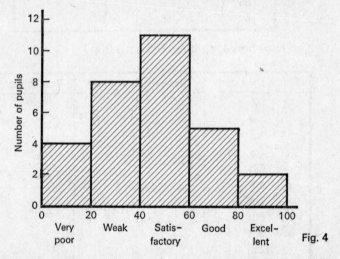

Fig. 4

Use this bar chart to help you to complete a copy of the table below (In the table the running total column has been given its technical name, *cumulative frequency* column. The word 'cumulative' is related to the word 'accumulate' which means to pile up.)

Marks	Number of pupils (frequency)	Running total (cumulative frequency)
0–20		
21–40		
41–60		
61–80		
81–100		

(a) Use the cumulative frequency column to find how many candidates gained

(i) 40 marks or less;   (ii) 80 marks or less.

(*b*) Can you use the table to find exactly the number of pupils gaining 75 marks or less? Can you estimate the number?

(*c*) How many pupils took the examination?
Can you estimate the median from the bar chart in Figure 4?
Can you estimate the median from the table?

4. CUMULATIVE FREQUENCY CURVES

We could answer the questions in (*b*) and (*c*) more easily by using the cumulative frequency table to draw a *cumulative frequency curve* (see Figure 5).

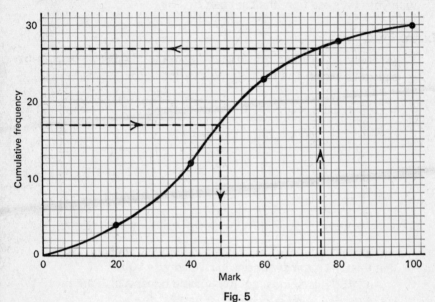

Fig. 5

Compare the plotted points with the entries in the cumulative frequency table. Notice how each cumulative frequency is plotted at the end of its corresponding interval (for example, 20 marks or less is plotted at 20, 40 marks or less is plotted at 40, etc.). This is because it is only at the end of an interval that we can be sure that all the members of the interval are accounted for.

(*a*) Since 30 pupils took the examination, the median mark is the mark half-way between the 15th and 16th values. Use the cumulative frequency curve to estimate the value of the median mark. (The dotted lines have been drawn to help you.)

(*b*) Use the second pair of dotted lines to estimate how many pupils gained 75 marks or less.

(*c*) Approximately how many pupils gained 30 marks or less?

151

4.1 The true median

The actual marks, arranged in ascending order, from which the bar chart in Figure 4 was obtained are:

8, 14, 17, 20, 22, 23, 24, 28, 32, 32, 34, 36, 44, 44, 44,

45, 47, 47, 51, 53, 54, 57, 60, 61, 61, 62, 72, 80, 91, 93.

Work out the true median. Compare it with your estimated value. Do you think your estimate is reasonably accurate?

How many pupils gained 75 marks or less? How does this compare with your estimate from the bar chart?

Exercise C

1 A survey was carried out to investigate the number of eggs in tree-sparrows' nests. The table shows the findings.

Number of eggs	Frequency	Cumulative frequency
2	2	
3	7	
4	25	
5	53	
6	12	
7	1	

Copy and complete the cumulative frequency column. Do you agree that the total number of nests inspected was 100?

With 100 nests, there are two middle ones. Which are they? What is the median number of eggs per nest?

Find also the modal and mean number of eggs in a nest. Compare the three averages.

2 Copy and complete the cumulative frequency column for the information in the following table and then draw a cumulative frequency curve. Find the median mark as accurately as you can from your graph. How many candidates got

(a) 35 marks or less;

(b) 65 marks or less;

(c) 82 marks or less?

If the pass mark was 45%, how many candidates

(i) passed;   (ii) failed?

Does the total of those who passed and those who failed equal 550?

Marks in test	Number of pupils	Cumulative frequency
0–10	3	
11–20	17	
21–30	41	
31–40	85	
41–50	97	
51–60	115	
61–70	101	
71–80	64	
81–90	21	
91–100	6	

3   A competition at a school fete involved guessing how many marbles there were in a glass jar. 499 people took part and the table below shows how their guesses were grouped. The correct answer was 447. Draw a cumulative frequency curve and estimate how near the median guess was to the correct answer. Did the competitors tend to 'under guess' or 'over guess'?

Number of marbles	Number of competitors
251–300	7
301–350	28
351–400	83
401–450	170
451–500	99
501–550	72
551–600	30
601–650	10

4   The following table shows the distribution of the number of full days' work lost through illness or strikes among 2000 factory employees.

Number of days	Number of employees
1–5	550
6–10	658
11–15	383
16–20	189
21–25	102
26–30	87
31–35	31
over 35	0

Draw a cumulative frequency curve and from it estimate the median number of days' work lost.

4.2 The true plotted points for continuous information

So far in this section we have dealt only with discrete information. If the numbers on the axis across the page in Figure 6 represented continuous information, for example, distances cycled in km instead of marks, then the true plotted points should be (20·5, 4), (40·5, 12), (60·5, 23), (80·5, 28), (100·5, 30). See Figure 6.

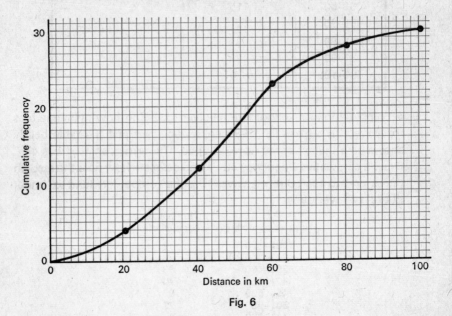

Fig. 6

Suppose you had cycled 20·1 km. This is 20 km to the nearest kilometre, and so would be placed in the 0–20 interval. The same is true for 20·49 km. However, if you had cycled 20·6 km, which is 21 km to the nearest kilometre, this would be placed in the 21–40 interval.

It is therefore only at 20·5 km that we can be sure to have included all the members of the 0–20 interval.

Into which interval would you place 40·499 km?

Into which interval would you place 40·503 km?

Compare Figures 5 and 6. Since there is practically no difference between them, it is not always worthwhile to plot points at the true end of the intervals when you are dealing with continuous information.

Exercise D

1 Draw a cumulative frequency curve for the set of weights of pupils shown in the table at the top of p. 155.

Weights of pupils in kg	Number of pupils	Cumulative frequency
40–45	1	
46–50	0	
51–55	3	
56–60	4	
61–65	7	
66–70	10	
71–75	15	
76–80	3	
81–85	1	

From your graph, write down the median weight of the class.

How many of the pupils weighed less than:

(*a*) 53 kg;   (*b*) 57 kg;   (*c*) 66 kg?

2   The table shows the length of life of 400 electric light bulbs. Draw a cumulative frequency graph for this information.

Length of life (hours)	Number of bulbs
200–299	10
300–399	26
400–499	32
500–599	60
600–699	88
700–799	76
800–899	62
900–999	34
1000–1099	12

How many bulbs did not last for:

(*a*) 250 hours;   (*b*) 725 hours?

From your graph write down the median life of the bulbs.

3   A 2 kg bag of new potatoes is found to contain 45 potatoes, with a distribution of weights as follows:

Weight (g)	1–20	21–40	41–60	61–80	81–100	101–120
Frequency	11	19	7	4	3	1

Draw up a table showing cumulative frequencies. What is the median interval?

Draw a cumulative frequency curve and hence find a better estimate of the median which will, of course, be in the median interval.

Estimate the mean and compare it with the median.

Puzzle corner

1 Write down seven 4's so that they add up to one hundred.

2 A water lily in a pond doubles its size every day and in 28 days it fills the whole pond. How long does it take to fill half the pond?

3 Arrange sixteen matches as shown in Figure 1. Remove four matches so as to leave only four small triangles. (No other matches may be moved and no loose ends left.)

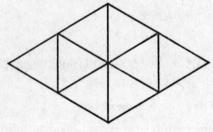

Fig. 1

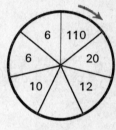

Fig. 2

4 Find the missing number in Figure 2.

5 Picking up the jumbled daily paper you notice that page 19 is missing. The back page is numbered 32. What other pages must be missing?

6 This simple subtraction uses all the digits from one to nine. Can you fill in the missing numbers? (There are two possible solutions.)

$$\begin{array}{r} 9 \quad . \quad . \\ - \; . \quad 4 \quad . \\ \hline . \quad . \quad 1 \end{array}$$

7 A lady handed a £1 note over the Post Office counter and asked for some 2p stamps, ten times as many 1p stamps and the remainder in 5p stamps. How can the clerk fulfil this request without giving her any change?

8 After collecting 385 conkers, three small boys divide them up so that the ratio of the number of conkers to age is the same for each boy. Every time Alan takes four conkers, Bob takes three, and for every six that Alan receives, Charles takes seven. How many conkers does each boy get?

9   Take a piece of paper 10 cm long and 2 cm wide and cut it into five pieces which can be rearranged to form a square.

10 Rearrange the counters in Figure 3 (*a*) to make the formation shown in Figure 3 (*b*). What is the minimum number of moves in which this can be done? (The numbers on the counters are just to help you describe the moves which you make with the counters.)

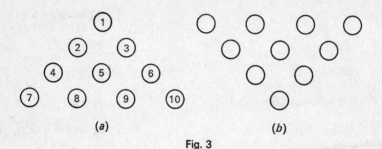

(*a*)   (*b*)

Fig. 3

11 A girl has a number of small boxes to pack into parcels. If she packs 2, 3, 4, 5 or 6 in a parcel she is left with one over. If she packs 7 in a parcel none are left over. What is the minimum number of boxes she can have to pack?

12 A man owns a square field containing a house and ten trees (see Figure 4). He offers it to his five sons on condition that they all live together in the house and divide the land into five equal plots, each plot being the same shape and containing two trees. How can this be done?

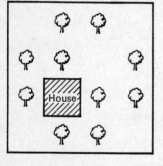

Fig. 4   Fig. 5

13 Use a pencil to copy Figure 5. Notice that there are only two rows with three dots in a line. Rub out one dot and draw it elsewhere so that there will be four rows of three-in-a-line.

Revision exercises

Computation 5

1 15×99.

2 $2\frac{1}{3} - 1\frac{1}{4} + \frac{3}{8}$.

3 $6536 \div 0 \cdot 38$.

4 The value of $13 \times \cos 13°$.

5 $^-8(3 - {}^-5)$.

6 $\begin{pmatrix} 6 & ^-5 \\ 4 & ^-3 \end{pmatrix} - \begin{pmatrix} 5 & ^-5 \\ ^-2 & 4 \end{pmatrix}$.

Computation 6

1 $35 \cdot 9 - 27 \cdot 6 - 5 \cdot 7$.

2 $1 \cdot 7 \times 936$.

3 $(40)^3$.

4 $\frac{4}{16} \div \frac{2}{3}$.

5 $72 \div (0 \cdot 6 \times 0 \cdot 3)$.

6 $\dfrac{10 \cdot 8 \times 0 \cdot 2}{0 \cdot 18 \times 1 \cdot 2}$.

Slide Rule Session No. 3

1 $0 \cdot 77 \times 141$.

2 $0 \cdot 91 \div 1 \cdot 8$.

3 $2110 \times 0 \cdot 089$.

4 $\sqrt{150}$.

5 $\pi \times (2 \cdot 15)^2$.

6 $(0 \cdot 36)^3$.

7 $\sqrt{(14 \times 33)}$.

8 $1 \cdot 23 \times 23 \cdot 4 \times 345$.

9 $\dfrac{66 \times 3 \cdot 35}{47 \cdot 2}$.

10 $\dfrac{8 \cdot 5}{26 \times 0 \cdot 75}$.

Exercise K

1 What is the sum of the angles of a hexagon?

2 Write down the exact square roots of:

(a) 4900; (b) $\frac{1}{4900}$; (c) $0 \cdot 0001$; (d) $0 \cdot 81$.

3 In an examination a boy obtained $\frac{17}{40}$. What percentage is this?

4 What base is being used if $35 + 43 = 122$?

5 Draw a Schlegel diagram for a tetrahedron.

6 Calculate the arithmetic mean of

(a) 1, 3, 5, 11, 2, 8;   (b) 815, 818, 814, 817, 816, 810, 822.

7 Without drawing the network, describe the order of the nodes of the network represented by

$$\begin{array}{c} \\ A \\ B \\ C \\ D \end{array} \begin{array}{c} A\ \ B\ \ C\ \ D \\ \begin{pmatrix} 2 & 0 & 1 & 1 \\ 0 & 0 & 3 & 0 \\ 1 & 3 & 0 & 1 \\ 1 & 0 & 1 & 2 \end{pmatrix} \end{array}.$$

8 A group of 540 students could study either French, German or Spanish. 246 pupils chose French, 165 chose German and 129 chose Spanish. Their choices are to be represented on a pie chart. How many degrees should be allocated to each subject?

Exercise L

1 What is the order of rotational symmetry of each of the following figures?

(a) Equilateral triangle; (b) regular hexagon; (c) parallelogram.

2 A is the set of prime factors of 24. List the members of A. What is $n(A)$?

3 Give an example of a number which is both a triangle and a square number.

4 Calculate the following:

(a) $146_{\text{eight}} + 22_{\text{eight}}$;   (b) $11010_{\text{two}} \div 10_{\text{two}}$.

5 Find the x- and y-coordinates of the points X, Y, Z in Figure 1.

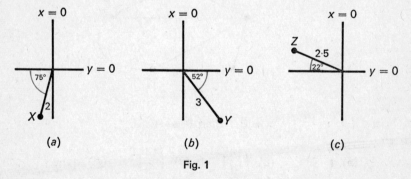

Fig. 1

6 Solve the following equations:

(a) $\dfrac{7}{x} = 14$;   (b) $\dfrac{4}{x} + 5 = 6$;   (c) $8 - \dfrac{3}{x} = 2$.

7   The volume of a cylinder is 156 cm³ and the area of its base is 13 cm².
What is the height of the cylinder?

8   In an examination 25% of the candidates failed. It is known that 99
candidates passed. How many took the examination?

Exercise M (Multi-choice)

In this exercise there may be more than one correct answer to a question.
Write down the letter (or letters) corresponding to the correct answer
(or answers). Show any rough working that you do.

1   A man's annual salary of £1000 is increased by 10% and then a month
later the new salary is increased by a further 10%. His annual salary
is now

(a) £1100;   (b) £1200;   (c) £1210;   (d) £1250.

2   Which of these is a fraction lying between $\frac{1}{4}$ and $\frac{2}{5}$?

(a) $\frac{1}{3}$;   (b) $\frac{1}{5}$;   (c) $\frac{1}{2}$;   (d) $\frac{2}{7}$.

3   Figure 2 shows a topological map of the roads connecting five
towns, A, B, C, D and E. Which of the following statements *may not*
be true?

(a) There is a direct route from B to C.

(b) E is nearer to D than to B.

(c) Four roads meet at E.

(d) The road from A to C passes through at least one other town.

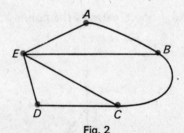

Fig. 2

4   If $\begin{pmatrix} 2 & -4 \\ 5 & 3 \end{pmatrix}\begin{pmatrix} 3 \\ -2 \end{pmatrix} = \mathbf{B}$, then **B** is

(a) $\begin{pmatrix} -2 \\ 9 \end{pmatrix}$;   (b) $\begin{pmatrix} 14 \\ 21 \end{pmatrix}$;   (c) $\begin{pmatrix} 14 \\ 9 \end{pmatrix}$;   (d) none of these.

5   The area of an island represented on a map of scale 1 to 1000 is 20 cm².
On a map of scale 1 to 200 its area would be

(a) 400 cm²;   (b) 500 cm²;   (c) 100 cm²;   (d) none of these.

6 Two cards are drawn at the same time from a full pack of fifty-two. The probability of drawing two picture cards is

(a) $\frac{12}{52}$;　(b) $\frac{24}{104}$;　(c) $\frac{144}{2652}$;　(d) $\frac{132}{2652}$.

Exercise N

1 A greengrocer buys a box of 40 pineapples for £5·60. Five of them go bad before he can sell them and have to be thrown away. The greengrocer sells the remaining pineapples for 20p each.

(a) What percentage of the pineapples did he have to throw away?

(b) How much money did the greengrocer take for the pineapples he did sell?

(c) What profit did he make?

(d) Write the profit as a fraction of the price the greengrocer gave for the box of pineapples.

(e) Change this fraction to a percentage to find his percentage profit.

2 Write down the values of the following:

(a) $\sin 125°$;　　　(b) $\sin 222°$;　　　(c) $\sin 336°$;

(d) $\cos 161°$;　　　(e) $\cos 288°$;　　　(f) $\cos 215°$.

3 Draw flow diagrams to solve each of the following equations:

(a) $\dfrac{8}{x} = {}^-2$;　　(b) $\dfrac{5}{x}+3 = 5$;　　(c) $\dfrac{3}{x}-6 = {}^-3$;

(d) $5+\dfrac{4}{x} = 6$;　　(e) $7-\dfrac{12}{x} = 10$;　　(f) $15-\dfrac{18}{x} = 6$.

4 A factory production line aims to produce 250 finished cars per shift. The following table summarizes the number produced in the 500 shifts that were worked in the first half-year.

Number of cars	Frequency
51–100	3
101–150	18
151–200	41
201–250	382
251–300	45
301–350	11

(a) Work out a cumulative frequency column.

(b) Draw a cumulative frequency curve and from it estimate the median number of finished cars per shift.

(c) How does this number compare with the target number of 250?

(d) Do you think that the factory had a good labour relations record? What could account for so many shifts falling way below the target number?

5 The two cones in Figure 3 are similar.

(a) If the diameter of the circular base of the smaller cone is 6 cm, what is the diameter of the base of the larger one?

(b) What is the ratio of their diameters?

(c) What is the ratio of (i) their surface areas; (ii) their volumes?

(d) If the volume of the larger cone is 254 cm³ to 3 S.F., use your slide rule to calculate the volume of the smaller one.

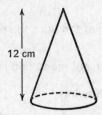

Fig. 3

6 Make a table of values for $y = x^2 - 3$ for values of x between $^-4$ and 4 and draw the graph. Use your graph to find

(a) the value of y when $x = ^-1 \cdot 3$;

(b) the values of x when $y = 4 \cdot 5$;

(c) the solutions of $x^2 - 3 = 10$.

Exercise O

1 (a) A car which costs £1000 when new decreases in value by 20% during the first year. What is the value of the car at the end of the first year?

(b) In each subsequent year the decrease is 10% of the value of the car at the beginning of that year. What is the value of the car at the end of the second year?

(c) What is the value of the car at the end of the third year?

(d) The buyer makes a hire purchase agreement by which he pays £250 as a deposit and then £25 a month for three years. How much interest does he pay over the three years? Express the interest as a percentage of the loan.

2 Figure 4 shows a Big Wheel at a fair with twelve seats equally spaced around it. The wheel rotates in an anticlockwise direction and is of radius 20 m. Amy is sitting in the seat marked *A* and Bridget in the seat marked *B*. Amy's seat is 1 m above the ground.

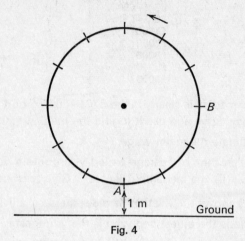

Fig. 4

(*a*) Through how many degrees must the wheel rotate before Bridget is vertically above Amy? When does this happen again? Is Amy ever vertically above Bridget and, if so, when does this first happen?

(*b*) Make a scale drawing of the wheel on graph paper using a radius of 4 cm. Use the drawing to help you draw the graph of the relation between the angle turned through (with the starting position as shown in Figure 4) and the height of the seat *A* above the ground. The table for the graph will start:

Angle turned through in degrees	0	30	
Height of *A* above ground in m	1		

(*c*) On the same axes, draw the graph of the relation for seat *B*.

(*d*) What can you say about the point where the two curves cross?

3 Solve each of the following equations:

(*a*) $\dfrac{16}{x} + 7 = 11$; (*b*) $\dfrac{3}{x} = {}^-9$; (*c*) $14 - \dfrac{24}{x} = 2$;

(*d*) $11 - \dfrac{10}{x} = {}^-19$; (*e*) $3(7-x) = 12$; (*f*) $4 - \tfrac{1}{3}x = 7$;

(*g*) $5(7-2x) = 10$; (*h*) $\dfrac{1}{2}\left(6 - \dfrac{18}{x}\right) = 6$.

4 A small factory has 200 employees and the annual wage bill is distributed as follows:

Wage	Number of employees
£501–£700	35
£701–£900	90
£901–£1100	30
£1500	28
£2000	10
£3000	3
£5000	3
£8000	1

(*a*) The median is clearly in the £701–£900 group. Draw a cumulative frequency curve and use it to find the median more accurately.

(*b*) Estimate the mean wage.

(*c*) Which form of average would you quote if you were (i) a shop steward, (ii) the managing director? Give reasons for your answers.

5 Figure 5 shows the relation 'is older than' on a set of four children.

(*a*) Who is the oldest and who is the youngest?

(*b*) Write down a matrix which represents the relation shown in Figure 5. Call it **O**.

(*c*) Write down the transpose of **O**. What relation does it represent?

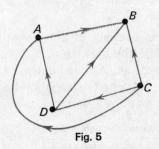

Fig. 5

6 On squared paper, draw the triangle T_1, whose vertices are $(1, 1)$, $(4, 2)$, $(4, 4)$. (Allow for values of x between $^-5$ and 10 and values of y between $^-3$ and 8.)

(*a*) The translation with vector $\begin{pmatrix} -5 \\ -3 \end{pmatrix}$ maps T_1 onto T_2. Draw and label triangle T_2.

(*b*) The vector $\begin{pmatrix} -5 \\ -3 \end{pmatrix}$ maps T_3 onto T_1. Draw and label triangle T_3.

(*c*) Write down the vector of
  (i) the translation which maps T_2 onto T_3;
  (ii) the inverse translation which maps T_3 onto T_2.

(*d*) Write down a pair of translations which have the same effect as the translation $\begin{pmatrix} -5 \\ -3 \end{pmatrix}$.

Exercise P

1 Find a rough answer and then use a slide rule to find the approximate values of each of the following:

(*a*) $\dfrac{1}{3 \cdot 7}$;

(*b*) $\dfrac{1}{8 \cdot 3}$;

(*c*) $\dfrac{1}{7 \cdot 2}$;

(*d*) $\dfrac{1}{35}$;

(*e*) $\dfrac{1}{0 \cdot 15}$;

(*f*) $\dfrac{5}{6 \cdot 1}$;

(*g*) $\dfrac{17 \cdot 6}{3 \cdot 8}$;

(*h*) $0 \cdot 4 \times \dfrac{1}{6 \cdot 9}$;

(*i*) $\frac{1}{9} \div 46$;

(*j*) $\frac{1}{20} \div 13 \cdot 7$;

(*k*) $3 \cdot 5 \times 4 \cdot 7 \times \frac{1}{6}$;

(*l*) $(42 \div 66) \times \frac{1}{4}$.

2 Write a program to compute S where $S = \frac{44}{7}(r^2 + rh)$. (Start with inputs of r and h to stores A and B, respectively.)

The formula $S = \frac{44}{7}(r^2 + rh)$ gives the approximate surface area, S, of a closed cylinder. Use it to find the surface area of a closed cylinder or radius 3 cm and height 11 cm.

3 $A = \{$square, rectangle, rhombus, parallelogram, arrowhead, kite, trapezium$\}$.

(*a*) List the members of P, the subset of A, which possess line symmetry.

(*b*) List the members of Q, the subset of A, which possess rotational symmetry.

(*c*) List the members of $P \cap Q$.

4 Rain falls on a flat roof of area 44 m² and drains off into an empty cylindrical tank 2 m in diameter. Find the depth of the water in the tank after a rainfall of 1 cm. (Hint: start by finding the volume of rain that falls.)

5 Triangle ABC has coordinates $A(-1, 2)$, $B(-2, 0)$, $C(-1, 0)$ and triangle XYZ has coordinates $X(1, 2)$, $Y(2, 0)$, $Z(1, 0)$. Draw these triangles on graph paper.

(*a*) Describe a single transformation which will map ABC onto XYZ.

(*b*) Describe two transformations which, taken in turn, will map *ABC* onto *XYZ*.

(*c*) On your diagram show the image of triangle *ABC* after the transformation represented by the matrix $\mathbf{S} = \begin{pmatrix} 1 & -1 \\ 1 & 1 \end{pmatrix}$.

Label the image $A_1B_1C_1$.

(*d*) Repeat (*c*) for the matrix $\mathbf{T} = \begin{pmatrix} \frac{1}{2} & \frac{1}{2} \\ -\frac{1}{2} & \frac{1}{2} \end{pmatrix}$.

Label this image $A_2B_2C_2$.

(*e*) Calculate **ST** and **TS**. What can you say about **S** and **T**?

(*f*) Without any further calculation, state the image of $A_1B_1C_1$ after the transformation represented by **T**.

6   Figure 6, not drawn to scale, shows a crankshaft, *AB*, which is attached at *A* to the rotating arm *CA*. *B* slides along *PQ*.
   If *CA* = 1 m and *AB* = 5 m, calculate

(*a*) the maximum and minimum distances of *B* from *C* as the arm rotates;

(*b*) the distance *CB* when the arm, *CA*, is vertical;

(*c*) angle *ABC* when the arm, *CA*, is vertical.

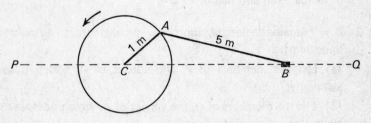

Fig. 6

Exercise Q

1   A boy takes two 10 cm rods and two 6 cm rods and fastens them together at their ends so as to form a quadrilateral. Sketch and name all the possible quadrilaterals he could make and describe the symmetries of each.

2   How many diagonals can be drawn from one vertex of an *n*-sided polygon?
   How many diagonals does an *n*-sided polygon have altogether?

3 (*a*) Transform the square in Figure 7 by the matrix

$$\begin{pmatrix} -\frac{3}{5} & \frac{4}{5} \\ \frac{4}{5} & \frac{3}{5} \end{pmatrix}.$$

Label the image $L_1 M_1 N_1 O_1$.

(*b*) Use tracing paper to check that $L_1 M_1 N_1 O_1$ is the same size and shape as *LMNO*.

(*c*) Draw the line $y = 2x$. If you folded your paper along this line, what would happen? Describe carefully the transformation which is represented by

$$\begin{pmatrix} -\frac{3}{5} & \frac{4}{5} \\ \frac{4}{5} & \frac{3}{5} \end{pmatrix}.$$

(*d*) Write down the inverse of

$$\begin{pmatrix} -\frac{3}{5} & \frac{4}{5} \\ \frac{4}{5} & \frac{3}{5} \end{pmatrix}.$$

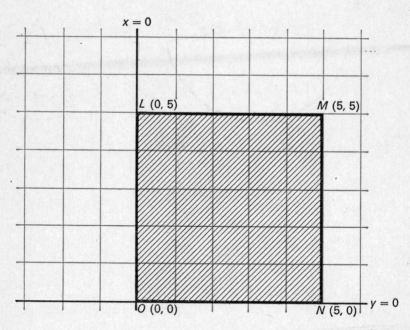

Fig. 7

4 Find the surface area of a regular octahedron whose edges are 14 cm long. (Hint: use Pythagoras's rule to find the height of a triangular face.)

5 (*a*) Is it possible to shear a square into a rhombus (a parallelogram with four equal sides) keeping one side of the square fixed? Draw a diagram *either* to show how to make the shear *or* to help explain why it is impossible.

(*b*) Repeat (*a*) for a parallelogram in which a long side is kept fixed.

6 The curved surface of a conical tent is a sector of a circle, radius 2·5 m, angle 160° (see Figure 8).

(*a*) The length of the arc of the sector equals the circumference of the base of the tent. Write down expressions for both of these and so find the radius, *r*, of the circular base of the tent.

Now calculate:

(*b*) the area of the base;

(*c*) the height of the tent;

(*d*) the volume of the tent, given that the volume of a cone is

$$\tfrac{1}{3} \times \text{area of base} \times \text{height.}$$

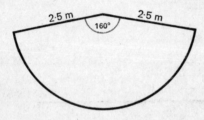 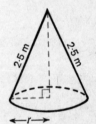

Fig. 8

Exercise R

Copy and complete this cross-number.

1.	2.		3.			4.	5.
6.		7.			8.		
	9.		10.		11.		
12.			13.	14.			15.
		16.					
	17.			18.	19.	20.	
21.					22.		23.
24.			25.			26.	

Clues across

1. The ninth prime number.
3. How many edges has a pentagonal prism?
4. $50 \times \cos 23 \cdot 1°$.
6. 11_{four} in base two.
8. 130_{twelve} in base ten.
9. The mean of $165 \cdot 1$, $157 \cdot 8$, $163 \cdot 2$, $160 \cdot 4$, $158 \cdot 3$, $161 \cdot 2$.
11. The symmetry number of a cube.
13. 60π to 3 s.f.
16. 65% of 240.
17. $23 \cdot 4 - 19 \cdot 6 - 14 \cdot 3 + 43 \cdot 5$.
18. A cube of side 4 cm is enlarged with scale factor 2. What is the volume of the enlargement (in cm³)?
21. $(^-2 \times \,^-50) - (^-3 \times 13)$.
22. The sum of the numbers in the 8th row of Pascal's triangle.
24. $^-9 + (^-7)^2$.
25. The volume of a cylinder (in cm³) of base area 5·5 cm² and height 8 cm.
26. $7 - \dfrac{100}{x} = 5$. What is the value of x?

Clues down

1. The area (in cm²) of a triangle of base 7 cm and height 6 cm.
2. The 151st odd counting number.
4. The 22nd square number.
5. $36 \div \frac{3}{5}$.
7. $18 \times \sin 65 \cdot 3°$ to 2 s.f.
8. The median of 127, 131, 133, 121, 134, 124, 133, 123.
10. Divide £184 in the ratio 3 to 5. What is the largest share (in £)?
12. $\sqrt{256}$.
14. $3460 \times 0 \cdot 25$.
15. How many sides has a dodecagon?
16. $10008 \div 72$.
17. The value of $3a(a-1)$ when $a = 11$.
19. The area of a circle is 132 cm². What is the area (in cm²) of a sector of this circle of angle 30°?
20. The half-way value of the group 200–250.
21. $\frac{1}{2}x - 2 = 5$. What is the value of x?
23. $A = ab - 5a$. What is b when $A = 150$ and $a = 2$?

Published by the Syndics of the Cambridge University Press
Bentley House, 200 Euston Road, London NW1 2DB
American Branch: 32 East 57th Street, New York, N.Y.10022

© Cambridge University Press 1971

Library of Congress Catalogue Card Number: 68-21399

ISBNs: 0 521 08161 0 limp covers
       0 521 08362 1 hard covers

First published 1971
Reprinted 1972

Printed in Great Britain
at the University Printing House Cambridge
(Brooke Crutchley, University Printer)